Swimming against the tide

Polarisation or progress on 20 unpopular council estates, 1980-1995

Anne Power and Rebecca Tunstall

July 1995

© Joseph Rowntree Fo

All rights reserved

Published by
Joseph Rowntree Fou
The Homestead
40 Water End
York YO3 6LP
Tel: 01904 629241

ISBN 1 85935 009 7
Price £9.00

Designed by Peter Adkins Design
Printed by Ryedale Printing, Kirkbymoorside

Printed on recycled paper

JR
JOSEPH
ROWNTREE
FOUNDATION

Contents

Acknowledgements   3

Summary   4

1
Introduction   7

2
Method   10

3
About the estates   12

4
Polarisation on estates: the evidence   15

5
Progress on estates: the evidence   36

6
A change in direction: estate trajectories   63

7
Conclusions and recommendations   69

Appendix tables   76

Notes   80

Bibliography   81

List of figures and tables   83

Acknowledgements

We would like to thank all the residents and staff in the 18 local authorities involved in this study, including directors, area and estate staff. Without their help and co-operation we could not have collected the information about the estates. Health, police, youth, community, repairs and caretaking staff were also extremely helpful.

Many other people contributed to the project over the past two years, including Deborah Georgiou who devised the survey and carried out the initial visits, Josie Dixon who played a major part in the study, uncovering the Census information for the estates, Jane Dickson who meticulously, speedily and creatively prepared the text, tables and diagrams, Jheni Arboine and Paul Herrmann who took the photographs, David Darton and Richard Best of the Joseph Rowntree Foundation for help with publication, and Anne Green for her advice.

We would particularly like to thank Julie Fawcett of the Stockwell Park Estate, Alan Murie of Birmingham University, Michael Burbidge of the Department of Environment, Tricia Zipfel of the Priority Estates Project, Susan Angoy of the Deptford City Challenge, John Low of the Joseph Rowntree Foundation, and John Hills of the London School of Economics, for their important contributions to our thinking as members of our advisory group, for their comments on the report at many different stages, and for their insights into the problems we were trying to understand. A particular thanks to John Hills who edited the final version of the report.

The authors accept full responsibility for any mistakes or misinterpretations.

Summary

Over the 1980s, social polarisation - particularly in large unpopular council estates - became more extreme.

Twenty of the most difficult estates in England experienced a dramatic improvement in their conditions at the beginning of the 1980s under the impact of estate-based housing management offices and tenant involvement.

This report documents the radical changes over the 1980s from the perspective of staff and residents on these estates, presenting evidence of their social and housing conditions between 1980 and 1994.

The estates were spread across the country, and built at different times and in different styles. Two-thirds were flats and most were large, with around 1,000 units. As physical and social entities, the estates were cut off from the nearby cities.

Half the study local authorities were in London; the rest were mainly other major cities with declining populations.

Polarisation

- Social conditions on the estates deteriorated over the 1980s and polarisation by a number of Census measures was far more extreme in 1991 than in 1981.
- Unemployment levels on the estates were three times the national average in 1981 and 1991. Economic inactivity rose on the estates over the same period, whereas it fell nationally.
- The proportion of elderly people on the estates was lower than average and falling. The proportion of children and young people was far above average.
- The proportion of all households headed by a lone parent rose nationally from 3 to 4 per cent. In the study local authorities, it doubled from 3 to 6 per cent. On the 20 estates it rose from 9 to 17 per cent. On all estates, over one-third of families with children were headed by a lone parent, and on half the estates over 50 per cent of all families with children were lone-parent families.
- There was a sharp division between London and the rest of England in the concentration of minority ethnic groups on the estates. Outside London most estates were almost exclusively white, even in cities with significant minority ethnic populations. In London, generally, the concentration of minority ethnic groups on estates was much higher than the local authority average. On a majority of the London estates the proportion was over 45 per cent and on two it was over 60 per cent.
- Secondary schools serving the estates performed far worse than the national average. Less than half the national average proportion of children in estate-linked schools got five or more GCSE passes at A to C level. Four times the number of children from estate-linked schools got no GCSEs at all compared with the study local authorities as a whole.
- One in six pupils from estate-linked schools compared with one in eleven nationally were absent from school registration for any half-day session.
- The Right to Buy had led to the sale of a quarter of the national council stock. Sales had been slightly lower in the study local authorities. On the estates only 5 per cent of the stock had been sold to tenants. Overall the tenure of estates had changed significantly in very few cases.
- The fear of social breakdown resulting from the increasing concentration of needy and vulnerable households was so acute that special localised measures to reinforce community stability were constantly necessary.

Progress

- Local offices had remained open on 17 of the estates over the whole 15 years (with another estate served by a nearby office). They had acquired more decentralised functions, but also covered wider areas, including occasionally other large estates. More localised responsibility helped counteract the problem of greater size.

- Over the 15 years of localised, targeted effort, government and local authority programmes directed significant capital resources at these estates. Modern estates received the most, on average £13,000 a home. Older balcony block estates received on average only £700 per unit. Five of the estates were undergoing radical restructuring or replacement, costing between £30,000 and £85,000 a unit.

- Local managers found physical upgrading successful in three-quarters of cases. Residents' views were more mixed, but only in two cases did they regard improvements as unsuccessful.

- The volume of empty property had fallen on most estates to around 4 per cent. However, on five estates major lettings crises had led to up to 50 per cent of all properties being empty at particular times.

- Local lettings administration consistently led to less empty property over the whole 15 years. One-offer-only policies and centralised lettings led to more empty property.

- The turnover of population on the 20 estates had fallen but was generally higher than corresponding council averages.

- Arrears in numbers of weeks of rent owing had risen steeply on the London estates, but were now falling rapidly. Overall arrears levels were steady.

- The number of services and facilities on the estates had greatly increased over the 15 years. Resident involvement had also grown significantly. Three tenant management organisations were progressing towards tenant control.

- Crime was still a major problem and source of anxiety on most estates. Crime problems did not appear strongly related to design. Residents were even more worried than managers by the possibility of social breakdown. In spite of this, both residents and managers believed that crime was falling or steady in three-quarters of the estates.

- Most estates were still considered unpopular and stigmatised but in most cases they were no longer the most difficult areas within the study local authorities. Sixteen had been among the least popular in 1980. Now only eight were.

- Residents and managers believed that conditions on half the estates were continuing to improve. On six estates, previously improved conditions were being held with some difficulty. On four, conditions were deteriorating and the future viability of three estates was in question.

- The physical and management changes, coupled with community involvement in the estates, generally had positive impacts.

- A major reason for this success was the continual support and daily management input for a decade and a half from the local authority landlords. This had sustained improvements in a period of greatly worsening social pressures in the poorest communities which these estates typified.

Costs

- The cost of the intensive, localised staff inputs into the estates was estimated to be one-fifth of the full housing management cost per unit in the study local authorities.

Government policies

- Government policies have had a mixed impact on the estates. Sales had been limited on the estates, while many wider policies intensified polarisation. But Estate Action, support for resident involvement, and ring-fenced Housing

Revenue Accounts had all led to significant improvements.

- The introduction of Compulsory Competitive Tendering for estate maintenance and caretaking had worked reasonably but it was creating uncertainty for local housing managers, and the Single Regeneration Budget was undermining the estate focus. Both policies risked bypassing local communities and the benefits of estate-based intensive initiatives.

Conclusions

- The 20 estates in this survey were *not* uniquely difficult – social and management problems affect social housing generally. All large social housing estates need intensive management.
- Most estates stood out as public housing even after major improvements.
- Intensive localised management was as important in arresting decline as reinvestment.
- The long-standing estate bases allowed hands-on management control, but the growing social disadvantages created intense management pressure.
- Lettings worked better if they were locally run, encouraging community links and a stable social base.
- Residents were the linchpin of change. They supported strong local management control over conditions. They feared social breakdown and were less optimistic than managers over progress. Tenants could not generally take on full responsibility for managing their estates. But their involvement was a crucial factor in the progress we found. Other services could gain from localisation and involvement.
- Wider social and economic pressures pushed the most disadvantaged – often unemployed, lone parents, people from minority ethnic groups – to the most marginal areas. The polarisation was mitigated by upgraded conditions and local support, but wider action was needed, for example in schools.
- Joblessness was a chronic problem. To be viable, estates needed much more than local management.
- The police needed local bases and strong community links. Crime was not increasing on most estates. Young people were vital to success in overcoming crime problems. Government policies had mixed results, with more polarisation but more involvement and local management. New directions such as the Single Regeneration Budget and Compulsory Competitive Tendering may reduce tenant involvement and the estate focus.
- These estates need permanent local management if marginal communities are to work.

Recommendations

- Protect what works – keep estate bases.
- Localise other services.
- Integrate estates into the surrounding community.
- Support bottom-up *and* top-down structures.
- Make spending longer-term and slower.
- Allocate housing to more diverse groups.
- Control allocations to disruptive households.
- Build on youth and ethnic diversity in city regeneration.

1 Introduction

In 1994 there were nearly five million council homes in Britain, by far the largest stock of publicly owned and run housing in the Western world, most of it on large, separate, single class, single use estates.

This study follows the fate of 20 of the most difficult council estates through the 1980s and early 1990s. In 1994 we revisited them to see the effects of government and local authority action in a turbulent era. We spoke to residents and staff about conditions and changes. The estates had experienced the most extreme decline and the most radical approaches to rescue. They were a microcosm of social tensions and divisions, a litmus paper of polarisation and progress.

In 1979 when the Conservatives took office, these estates were rapidly becoming unlettable. There were simply not enough people willing to live on them, despite remarkably low rents and high amenities – they were far cheaper than most private alternatives, and had better internal conditions. There were many (at least 2,000) such estates all over the country.[1] No matter how big or difficult the estates (and most had between 500 and 1,000 units), with very few exceptions there was no locally-based service to run them, no role for tenants who wanted to be involved, and no proper repair programme.[2]

Our first visits in 1979 and 1980 revealed shocking conditions on most of the estates – dirty, chaotic, impoverished, vandalised, hard-to-let, unrepaired islands of neglect. Boarded-up properties, a massive exodus of tenants, very few if any trained staff, low demand, and no contact point between tenants and landlords, made the estates unpopular, vulnerable and sometimes out of control.[3]

Although the DoE's *Investigation of Difficult to Let Housing* was not yet published and the Priority Estates Project had only just begun, local authorities were already alarmed by these conditions. Extreme conditions on a handful of the most marginal estates catapulted local authorities into action. By 1980, 18 authorities in England were pushing bright, young, energetic catalysts to the front line. They set up *ad hoc* offices in empty shops or boarded-up houses; formal 'rules' did not matter – getting things done did. Locally based council 'entrepreneurs' brought action to the estates and turned wasteful paper-pushing into direct services.[4]

This approach transformed conditions quickly:

- lettings, repairs and caretaking were controlled by local managers;
- local managers were free to innovate;
- with strong political backing they could take immediate action, cutting through red tape;
- there was an open-door approach with tenants, giving their views priority;
- police were pressured into returning to the beat;
- committed, locally-based staff inspired confidence and generated action; local offices became the nexus of change.

Hundreds of new tenants' initiatives grew around these special projects. Gradual physical improvements resulted from the priority status given to these estates. By 1982, most of the 20 estates with local offices which we investigated (within these 18 local authorities) had improved almost beyond recognition through simple, localised measures, better tenant relations and a radically new management approach.[5]

Central government supported these initiatives because the vast, publicly owned stock was otherwise in danger of becoming an unmanageable and unsaleable liability. Fears of disorder grew as crime levels rose and major city areas broke into riots – London, Birmingham, Liverpool, and Bristol all experienced rioting in 1981–82. This spurred the national shift to local management, clearly more responsive to local communities than centralised bureaucracies. Nationally, decentralisation emerged as one of the most ambitious, but unplanned and unlegislated, housing reforms of the 1980s.[6]

Declining estates experienced tumultuous change alongside management reforms. They were close to the bottom of the social pecking order. The lack of formal jobs and rapid growth in lone parenthood increased dependence among council tenants. Concentrations of black people on unpopular estates grew, particularly in London. Exploding home ownership drew many stable households out of renting, turning estates into 'welfare islands' – most people on these estates could not buy even if they wanted to. The financial and social gap between council housing and the majority of the country increased rapidly,[7] and the worst estates were worse than most council housing.

About this report

This report sets out to capture how the changes since 1980 have affected the 20 estates originally visited and their residents. Did local housing management restore good conditions?

Did tenants want to participate and be involved? Could they actually make a difference? Was race an issue in inner cities? Were the police unpopular? Was crime worsening? Was money wasted on improving badly designed and built estates? Was the gap growing between these estates and the rest of the city? Had government sales policies failed? Were councils bad landlords? These were some of the recurring questions. More offensive questions were posed by hasty media pundits and politicians. Did lone parents have children in order to get council housing? Did the homeless queue-jump? Did idle and destructive young people not want to work? Was the threatened 'underclass' already a reality in Britain?[8]

The areas we visited were cut off from the rest of the city by poor transport, off-putting design and condition, lack of economic activity, and above all reputation. Our findings tell a story of largely separate development that is often misrepresented, exaggerated, distorted or buried, precisely because so few people, apart from residents and local workers, ever have to go to these estates. We present a view based on the direct experience of residents and staff working on the estates.

We tried to capture how the estates were changing. Changes over time highlight *patterns* of development that better define the shape of things than single snapshots. This closely focused picture of area change over the Conservative era 1980–95 clarifies from the bottom the way our cities are going. It examines the role of council landlords, residents and central government in tackling – or creating – the problems of the most marginal communities in the country over a 15 year period of promised progress and powerful polarisation.

Structure of the report

The opening summary briefly presents our findings, and this chapter introduces the themes of the report. Chapter 2 details how we carried out our research between 1980 and 1995. Chapter 3 gives background information on the 20 estates. Chapter 4 uses Census and other information to examine social polarisation on the estates over the 1980s. Chapter 5 looks at findings from our visits in 1981, 1987 and 1994, looking in particular at changes in housing management and conditions on the estates. Detailed information is in appendix tables. Chapter 6 brings this evidence together to present a picture of the estates' trajectories over the period. The conclusions and recommendations attempt to reconcile the complex trends and seemingly conflicting evidence, offering pointers for addressing serious new problems in marginal areas and highlighting our relative ignorance about the performance of the many high-cost services besides housing.

2

Method

This report is based on surveys of the same 20 estates conducted in 1981, 1987 and 1994. The estates were also visited in 1979 and 1980, before or at the start of the estate-based initiatives, providing valuable baseline evidence. This unique body of information allows us to examine not only conditions on the estates, but also the processes of change over fifteen years.[9] The first two surveys were funded by the Department of the Environment (DoE) as part of the Priority Estates Project (PEP). The third survey was funded by the Joseph Rowntree Foundation through the London School of Economics.

All bar three of the estate-based initiatives were set up independently of PEP and government, and funded by the local authorities, some with additional partnership funding through the Government's Inner Area Programme. All the estates were selected by their local authorities as in need of special measures to prevent conditions spiralling out of control. All the local authorities have participated in this study since 1981. The evidence in the surveys was collected directly from the local authorities and their employees working on the estates. All three surveys were the responsibility of Anne Power who visited the estates prior to and in the course of these studies. We interviewed locally-based staff in all offices in all three surveys. Interviews with staff were carried out by Margaret Pitt (1981), Brenda Jones (1987), and Rebecca Tunstall (1994), who visited and spoke to staff in all the offices. Some tenants and staff involved in 1981 were still on the estates and involved in 1994, lending some visits a special depth. Performance information was checked with official statistics.

The number of residents interviewed rose sharply over the surveys. In 1981, we interviewed five residents. In that first survey, our main aim was to find out how local offices were functioning and only a few had developed resident involvement very far. In 1987, we interviewed 54 residents in 15 estates and in 1994, 131 residents from 17 estates. In 1994 we also interviewed area managers and other estate-based workers, as well as directors of housing and senior staff. In the first study, we made 40 estate visits; in the second, 60; in the third, 84 (Appendix Table A1).

Figure 1 breaks down residents interviewed in 1994 by sex, ethnic origin, and age. The proportion of women was far higher than their numbers in the population, following the tradition of women's heavy involvement in home and community affairs.[10] Nearly 20 per cent were from minority ethnic groups, compared to 25 per cent for the estate populations as a whole. The representatives were disproportionately older than average – nearly half over 50 – whereas estate populations were far more youthful than the national population.

We interviewed residents in groups, based on their local organisations. In three estates where there were several groups, we spoke to all groups. The residents we met were on the whole active representatives of their community, so their views are those of a specially involved group. Nonetheless, their numbers, ethnic and social backgrounds made them very much part of the estate communities, making their perspective as community representatives both enlightening and special.

Other important sources of information were 1981 and 1991 Census data. These highlighted population changes, both for the local authorities as a whole and for the estates, over most of the period studied. Census data were easy to identify, with boundaries often coincided with Census enumeration districts. Although Census boundaries had changed, with the help of the local authorities we reconstructed the boundaries for 1981 in 1991, making the two sets of Census information comparable. Comparison data for all council tenants in the study local authorities was unobtainable.

We also used local authority and estate reports. The study was informed by continuing contact throughout the entire period with local authorities, central government and other agencies concerned with social housing estates, and by research carried out by Anne Power between 1987 and 1994 on European social housing estates.[11]

The three surveys are reports from on the ground. Where possible we collected measurable evidence, but many of the views we recorded reflected the opinions and attitudes of staff and tenants, rather than hard statistics. Much of what we were examining could only be described and assessed by those directly concerned. The report presents an overview of findings without indicating particular estates. No finding applies to all estates unless explicitly stated.

We also made observations during the visits in all three surveys, covering environmental conditions, the state of buildings, progress with improvement work, facilities and services, incidents, and informal meetings, and collected photographic records of the estates over the 15 years.

Information for such a long and decisive period is unusual; it reflects housing and social change over the entire Conservative period. By returning to the same areas with similar questions, we could observe developments and the impact of change in a way that would be much harder had we obtained information from different areas. These return visits provided many surprises. The outcomes were certainly not as foreseen, making the story of great relevance to those who are concerned with social as well as housing problems.

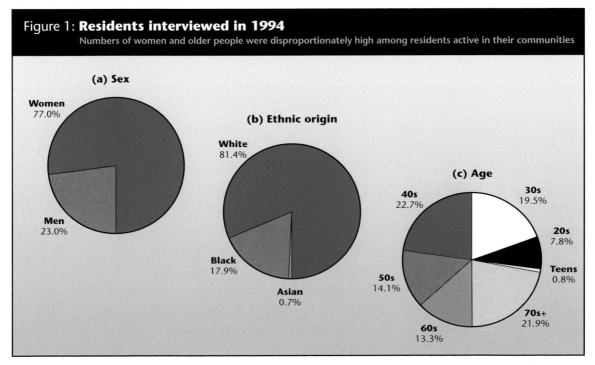

Figure 1: **Residents interviewed in 1994**
Numbers of women and older people were disproportionately high among residents active in their communities

(a) Sex
Women 77.0%
Men 23.0%

(b) Ethnic origin
White 81.4%
Black 17.9%
Asian 0.7%

(c) Age
40s 22.7%
30s 19.5%
20s 7.8%
Teens 0.8%
70s+ 21.9%
60s 13.3%
50s 14.1%

Notes: Ethnicity and age as assessed by interviewers.
Source: 131 residents interviewed in total.

3

About the estates

Table 1 summarises the style, age and size of the estates (for more detail see Appendix Table A2). Thirteen had over 800 units and six had over 1,200, but five were considerably smaller with under 500 units. The average size was 1,000.

The estates represented a broad range of building types and location. We divided them into three main designs:

Cottage estates: Mainly terraced, semi-detached, brick-built houses with gardens, built before World War II. These were often - though not always - smaller. All were outside London.

Balcony walk-up estates: Mainly inter-war or late 1940s blocks of flats, usually brick-built and under six storeys high. They were usually larger than cottage estates and were located in inner cities.

Modern concrete complex estates: Large-scale industrially built concrete estates of complex modernist design, usually with some high blocks, walkways, decks, underground garages and other now-unpopular features.

Figure 2 shows the average size of different types of estate. The modern concrete estates were generally by far the largest (all except one over 1,000 units), and also the most structurally distinct. All bar one of these were in London.

Figure 3 and Table 2 show the location of estates by design. They were spread all over

---

Table 1: **Size, style and age of the 20 estates**

	No. of estates	Type of estate		
		Cottage	Balcony	Modern
(a) Number of units				
250–500	5	4	1	0
501–800	2	0	2	0
801–1,200	7	2	1	4
1,201+	6	1	2	3
Total estates	20	7	6	7
(b) Type of building and age				
1930s	8	5	3	–
1940s	2	2	–	–
1940s/1950s	3	–	3	–
1960s	3	–	–	3
1970s	4	–	–	4
(c) High rise blocks				
with tower blocks over ten storeys	6	1	1	4
with high blocks over five storeys	10	1	2	7

Note: Several estates had a mix of design and ages. We classed them according to their dominant design.
Source: Local managers.

England from Tyneside, through Merseyside, Greater Manchester and the Midlands to London. A majority were in London, reflecting its greater concentration of council housing, high density of estates of flats, and problems.[12] Two-thirds of the estates comprised flats, whereas 60 per cent of council housing nationally comprises houses. The over-representation of flats in the sample reflects their generally lower popularity and greater management difficulties. It was originally a surprise[13] to find quite small brick-built cottage estates amongst the most difficult to let in the country. However, both government and local authority research has shown that estates with high levels of need, unpopular locations and poor management are prone to acute decline *even when containing potentially attractive houses with gardens.*[14]

The estates suffered from repetitive, utilitarian, collective design, mounting disrepair, unfavourable location, friction-prone layouts and strong stigma. The most serious problems in 1980 were:[15]

- neglected and rubbish-strewn environments;
- poor repairs and maintenance;
- difficulty in letting homes and a high level of empty property;
- high levels of crime and vandalism;
- far above average poverty, unemployment, child density, concentrations of lone parents and ex-homeless households;
- little community activity or involvement;
- in areas of ethnic settlement, a high concentration of minority ethnic groups. (see Table 28, p.65.)

All estates were part of major urban areas with large stocks of council housing. These cities lost population in the 1980s, some rapidly. The resulting drop in housing demand affected these estates, even in London where shortages were still common. Population loss was closely linked with job loss. In 1994, the vast majority

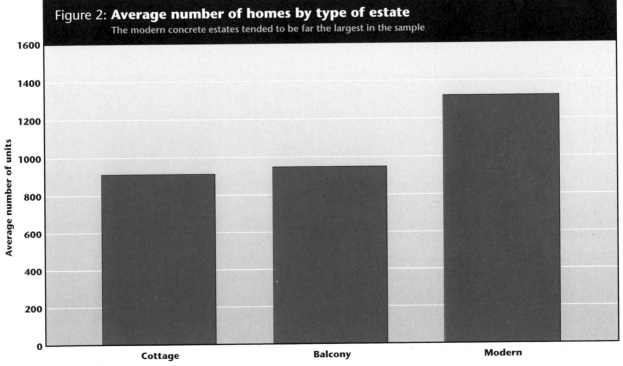

Figure 2: **Average number of homes by type of estate**
The modern concrete estates tended to be far the largest in the sample

Source: Local managers.

of residents were dependent on state benefits. The estates represented extreme concentrations of need, reflecting two decades of drastic economic change. Over the period, council housing as a whole changed from being a favoured solution, the hope of families in need, to being a last resort primarily for those squeezed out of the job market, private renting and the mainstream. As one Director put it, "It was a good thing to get a council flat in the 1970s. Now you have to be desperate."

Table 2: **Location of estates by design**			
Estate location	Number of estates		
	Total	Design	
		Flats	Cottage
London Inner	**8**	**11**	–
Outer	**3**		
Midlands	**2**	–	**2**
North West	**3**	**1**	**2**
Merseyside	**1**	**1**	–
North East	**3**	–	**3**
Total	**20**	**13**	**7**

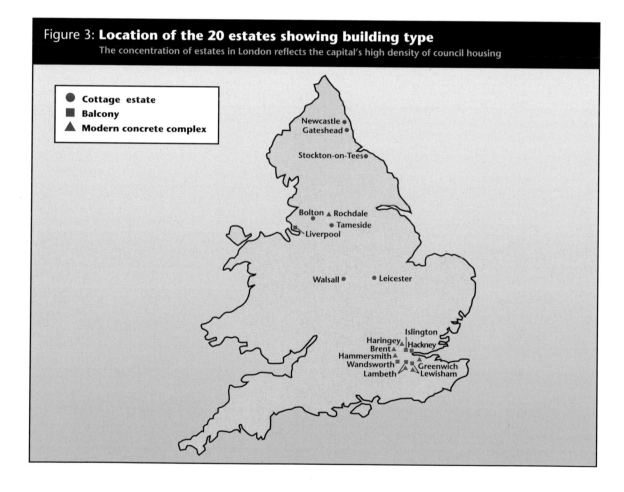

Figure 3: **Location of the 20 estates showing building type**
The concentration of estates in London reflects the capital's high density of council housing

● Cottage estate
■ Balcony
▲ Modern concrete complex

4

Polarisation on estates: the evidence

In this chapter we examine two of the most significant factors affecting the estates over the 1980s, changing social and economic conditions. In 1981, we asked the local authorities which problems had prompted unusual remedial action on these estates. Physical and management problems loomed large, but a dominant factor was the estates' extreme social polarisation. In 1980, they were far poorer than average, had much higher unemployment rates, more lone parents, more previously homeless families, and in London a higher proportion of minority ethnic groups. They housed much higher proportions of other vulnerable groups, had more young people, and far more social problems.[16]

Patterns of social decline

"Everyone with a young family and a little bit of intelligence wants to move off ... We're getting the waifs and strays." Resident

"You can hold a can of Special Brew and a spliff and walk around in front of the children without being ashamed – what kind of role model is that? 'Jones' to keep up with do help solve problems, but we haven't got any Jones ... there are so many irresponsible people here." Resident

Social problems could not be separated from building and organisational problems as they

---

Figure 4: **Outline patterns of social decline on estates**
Social problems on estates could not be separated from building or organisational problems

Poor physical and social conditions

Applicants with choice are deterred

Low social status of estates

Estates become harder to let

High turnover and vacancies

More vulnerable groups get housed

More difficulty in managing estates

More damage and disrepair

More unpopular - more exit

Lack of social cohesion

Breakdown in social controls

Difficulty in maintaining management control

Poorer conditions

Other services adversely affected

Chaotic conditions

Residents and local housing officer, North East.

"We go that extra mile, we don't just file complaints away; we don't just stick to housing duties… on Wednesday afternoon I answered the door seventeen times – when we're supposed to be closed." Local manager

were mutually reinforcing, as Figure 4 summarises. Poor physical and social conditions deterred applicants with more choice. The lower social status of the estates made them harder to let and keep occupied. High turnover and vacancies resulted in damage to buildings, loss of social cohesion and a breakdown in controls. These generated serious management problems, poorer conditions, deteriorating services and eventual chaos. It made the problems facing vulnerable households far more difficult to overcome.

By 1982 the intervention of a strong and localised management base had galvanised services, improved conditions and involved willing residents in restoring social controls on most estates.[17] This helped combat extreme social conditions, although it did not alter the distinct population composition. In 1987, this was still generally the case, but there was accumulated evidence of growing social problems on some estates and growing polarisation almost everywhere.[18] Local housing management was having to respond to social pressures far outside its normal brief, simply to maintain basic services. The process was like 'running to stand still'. The 1987 findings were borne out by the study of Priority Estates Projects by Howard Glennerster and Tessa Turner. They concluded that locally-based housing services were a necessary, but not sufficient, condition for improving estates.[19]

During 1994, we again collected resident and staff views on social problems and polarisation. The findings were somewhat contradictory. Fear of social breakdown had become a far more dominant issue, but was accompanied by some optimism about crime levels, estate conditions and management performance.

To assess more exactly the seriousness of social problems, we examined Census information for the estates in 1981 and 1991. In this way we were able to show the actual changes in population make-up, comparing the composition of the 20 estates with national figures and with figures for the whole population of the 18 local authorities where they were located (for a summary see Appendix Table A3). 1991 was the first year when a direct question on ethnicity was asked, but we were able to compare 1991 figures with earlier data on country of birth.

Population change

"There is no demand in the city."
Area manager

Between 1971 and 1981 the British population increased by 1 per cent, and between 1981 and 1991 by 2.5 per cent.[20] Apart from three northern authorities, the populations in the 18 local authorities we studied fell significantly to 1981 and continued falling, though generally more slowly, to 1991 (Table 3 and Appendix Table A4).

Table 3: **Study local authority population change 1971–91 (%)**		
	1971–81	1981–91
all study authorities (18)	**–10.7**	**–6.0**
London authorities (9)	**–14.7**	**–8.4**
inner urban authorities in North East and North West (3)	**–14.0**	**–9.4**
other authorities (6)	**–0.8**	**–0.7**

Note: For more details see Appendix Table A3.
Source: Census 1971, 1981 and 1991.

Urban population decline over two decades has removed many of the more economically active residents, weakened local economic, social and political structures, and reduced the employment and tax base of these urban areas. In the early

1970s, reducing the city population was a strong policy goal. It took time for the result to emerge as a problem. Population decline had a significant effect on housing demand, particularly for the least popular estates, as some filtering up into more attractive vacated housing occurred. As general housing market pressure declined and the supply of new houses continued to grow,[21] more viable households moved out of the estates, often out of the areas altogether. The great increase in household formation only partly made good the drop in demand.[22]

It is hard to overstate the long-term impact of these trends on cities (including London), on housing demand, and on the social composition of council housing.[23] If population decline continues in major cities, as it has done in the United States,[24] accelerated decay and eventual abandonment of the worst properties may become common.

Unemployment

The rate of unemployment in the 18 study local authorities was slightly above the national average in 1981 and 1991, but on the 20 estates it was over three times the national average (Figure 5). On 19 of the 20 estates, the unemployment rate was over 25 per cent in 1991 on Census definitions; on seven it was over 35 per cent. This extraordinarily high unemployment obviously affected income levels, but it also affected housing demand, as more active adults sought to leave. It affected internal patterns of behaviour, particularly among young people. Where work was scarce among adults, young people were less likely to undertake training, have access to employers, or even know how to go about finding work: *unemployment patterns could become self-reinforcing*. This in turn deterred more able and more dynamic applicants. Patterns of social decline were reinforced.

Economic inactivity

Adults who are neither employed nor registered as unemployed are classed as economically

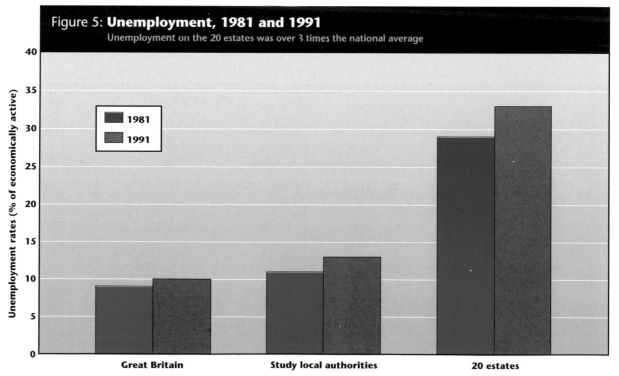

Figure 5: Unemployment, 1981 and 1991
Unemployment on the 20 estates was over 3 times the national average

Source: Census 1981 and 1991.

inactive. The level of economic inactivity had risen on 18 of the 20 estates alongside the rise in unemployment; by contrast, it fell slightly within the study local authority areas and nationally as women's employment rose (Figure 6). On the estates, inactivity rose because the opportunities for women working were more limited, and as longer-term unemployment eventually became converted into economic inactivity for many (people dropped off the dole queue). Male unemployment could also reduce a woman's incentive to take low-paid part-time work because benefit entitlement would be affected by income earned.[25] In poorer areas there is often an *increase* in both unemployment and economic inactivity in contrast to the national trends.[26]

In work

The combination of unemployment amongst the economically active and economic inactivity shows how seriously removed from the job market some communities are. On average *only 37 per cent* of adults on the 20 estates were in work in 1991, compared with 59 per cent for the study local authorities, and 58 per cent nationally (Figure 7). This gap helps to explain many other social problems.

Regional change – London and the rest of the country

The upper panel of Figure 8 ranks the 20 estates in order of unemployment in 1981, with the London estates concentrated on the left, other estates on the right. The lower panel shows the unemployment in the corresponding local authority areas. In 1981 there was a clear divide between most London estates with lower unemployment levels, and most other estates with extraordinarily high levels, and a much greater gap between out of London estates and their local authority areas.

Over the 1980s, the situation changed. Unemployment rose quickly in London and on the London estates. In five other (northern) authorities, it either remained static or fell, both

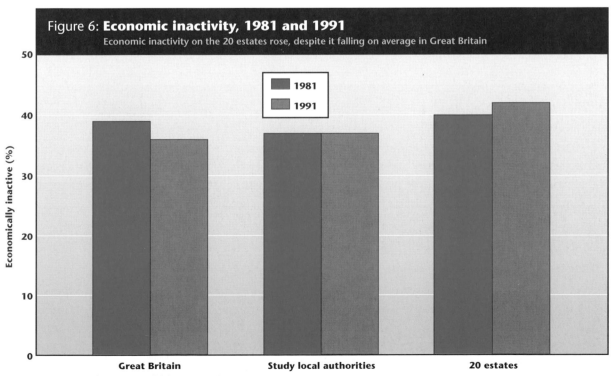

Figure 6: **Economic inactivity, 1981 and 1991**

Economic inactivity on the 20 estates rose, despite it falling on average in Great Britain

Note: Men and women aged 16+.
Source: Census 1981 and 1991.

19

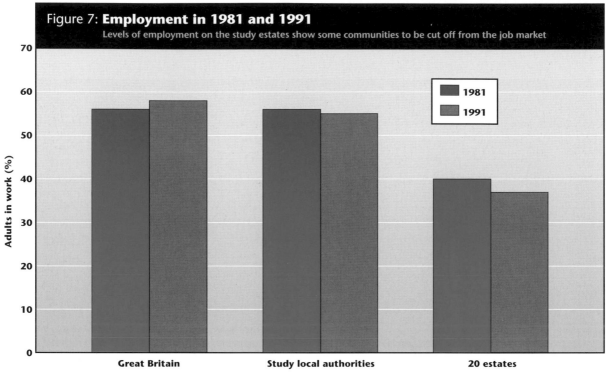

Figure 7: **Employment in 1981 and 1991**

Levels of employment on the study estates show some communities to be cut off from the job market

Adults in work (%)

1981
1991

Great Britain   Study local authorities   20 estates

Source: Census 1981 and 1991.

in the local authority area and on the estates. It is still a picture of stark contrast between the estates and their surrounding areas, but there is *a seriously worsening situation in London*.[27] The fall in unemployment on other (northern) estates is from such a high level that it still leaves them in a *generally worse position* than most of the London estates. By 1991 the levels were extraordinarily high on *all* estates, *over three times* the national average.

Children and young people

> *"There seem to be hundreds of lads on this estate ... The kids come out after 12 o'clock at night. The activity on this estate at 3 am is tremendous."* Resident

> *"Caretakers used to frighten the children in the old days – you can't look at a child now."* Resident

Council housing was primarily built for families with children. A very large majority of council dwellings have two or three bedrooms. On the 20 estates, over three-quarters of units were family-size.

Families with children have more urgent need for housing, take priority for social housing through homelessness legislation, and they generally have lower incomes. Out-of-work families, large families with three or more children, and lone-parent families are among the poorest groups.[28] They often have greater difficulty in gaining access to affordable housing. Councils have therefore, over time, housed disproportionate numbers of families with children, potentially or previously homeless households with children, and lone parents with children. All these pressures lead to far above the national average concentrations of children and young people on estates.

In 1981, one in five of the population nationally was under 16; on the estates it was close to one in three (31 per cent). By 1991, the national proportion of children had fallen slightly to 19 per cent, while the average on the estates was still 31 per cent. On two estates it was 43 per cent. The population aged under 24 on almost all the estates was still far above the national average. Overall, nearly half the estates' population was under 24 (Figure 9).

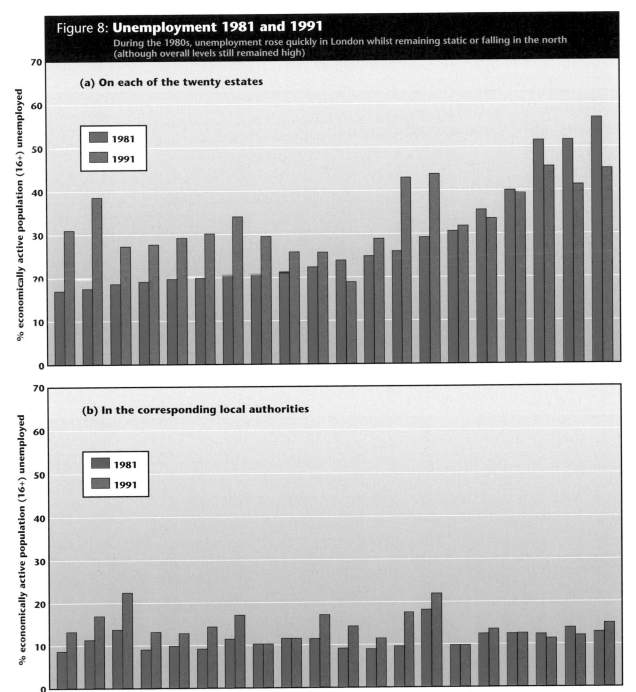

Figure 8: **Unemployment 1981 and 1991**
During the 1980s, unemployment rose quickly in London whilst remaining static or falling in the north (although overall levels still remained high)

(a) On each of the twenty estates

(b) In the corresponding local authorities

Note: Estates and their corresponding local authorities listed in order of increasing 1981 estate unemployment.
Source: Census 1981 and 1991.

Children's group at a multi-agency family and health project.

Longstanding resident, North West.

"We are tolerant of the pests we have now for fear of something worse" Resident

The existence of higher concentrations of young people helps to explain some of the estates' needs, management, and social problems. A major factor in their original decline was the presence of large numbers of young people. Young people are *not, of themselves, a problem*, but they are a serious responsibility.

The child population is dependent on families, and child-rearing is affected by poverty, unemployment, and family break-up. In teenage years, a youthful population is likely to cause vandal damage and other nuisance. One-third of young people commit a crime before the age of 18 and half of all recorded crimes are committed by a person under 21.[29]

Many implications flow from the youthful population of estates, affecting employment, housing management, repair, maintenance of common areas, policing, need for leisure facilities, schools, and so on. Extra demands are made on a wide range of services. But the young population is a large potential workforce and is at an active stage in family formation and child rearing.

Elderly people

In 1981 the average elderly population of the 20 estates was below the national average of 18 per cent (Figure 10). Only two estates had disproportionate concentrations with over 20 per cent. Sixteen estates had below the national average. By 1991, the national proportion had risen, but it fell on the estates as a whole, dropping slightly on 12 estates, and rising slightly on only four.

The exact cause of this fall is not clear, since the proportion of elderly people in council housing is generally high. Elderly people were moving off the estates, possibly to take up the now quite plentiful and attractive sheltered accommodation available in many local authorities, and away from areas with lots of noisy young people, nuisance, and other disturbance. Elderly tenants often felt insecure unless they had family members or other close links on the estates.

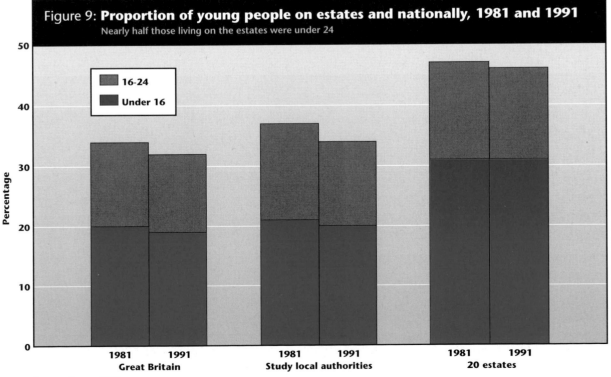

Figure 9: **Proportion of young people on estates and nationally, 1981 and 1991**
Nearly half those living on the estates were under 24

Legend:
- 16-24
- Under 16

Percentage (y-axis, 0 to 50)

1981 1991
Great Britain

1981 1991
Study local authorities

1981 1991
20 estates

Source: Census 1991.

23

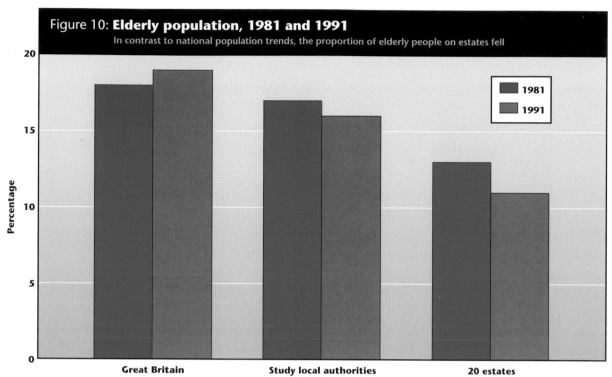

Figure 10: **Elderly population, 1981 and 1991**

In contrast to national population trends, the proportion of elderly people on estates fell

Note: Population aged 65+ (men) or 60+ women.
Source: Census 1981 and 1991.

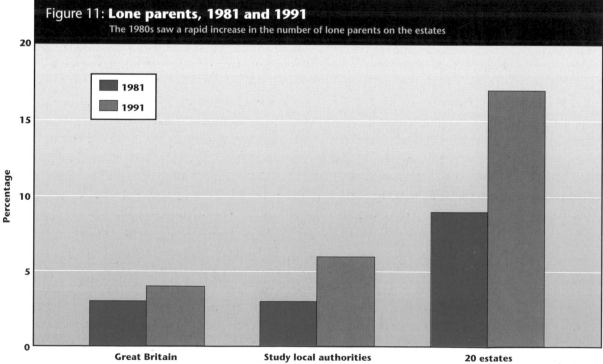

Figure 11: **Lone parents, 1981 and 1991**

The 1980s saw a rapid increase in the number of lone parents on the estates

Source: Census 1981 and 1991.

Many lettings policies militated against maintaining family links within council housing and therefore left elderly people sometimes feeling marooned and vulnerable on difficult estates.

Lone parents

One of the most dramatic and accelerating differences between the estates and elsewhere is the proportion of lone parents. Nationally, the proportion of households headed by lone parents has been rising fast. However, the concentration in council housing and on the 20 estates has grown far more rapidly. In 1981 there were already three times the level of lone parents on the estates than in the surrounding local authority areas (Figure 11). By 1991 the level both in the study local authorities and on estates had doubled. The gap between the estates and the rest had grown far larger.

The upper panel of Figure 12 shows the changes estate by estate, ranked according to the proportion of lone parents on the estates in 1981. The upper panel shows the scale of change, but also how varied and out of line are the extremes. Some of the estates with the lowest proportions in 1981 showed greatest increase. Most increased a great deal, in absolute terms by far more than in the corresponding local authorities shown in the lower panel.

On ten estates *over half of all families with children on at least two estates were headed by lone parents. On all the estates it was at least a third of all families with children.* This is three times the concentration in the population as a whole.

The concentration of lone-parent families, partly resulting from lettings priorities, is so significant as to have a major impact on estate conditions. The intensity of the concentration *reflects* the problems of unemployment and poverty, but it also *contributes to them.*

The combination of high unemployment, dependence on benefit, and lone parenthood can become mutually reinforcing. It is hard to know which is cause and which is effect in areas where so many pressures combine. From our survey, the critical finding was the extremely rapid increase in lone parenthood, more rapid and more consistent than any of the other changes.

Minority ethnic groups

Using Census figures for the number of residents in households with a head born in the New Commonwealth, in 1981 the study local authority areas generally had higher concentrations of minority ethnic households than the national average. Only three of the 18 authorities had significantly *below* the national average. Most were far above.

By 1991, the apparent concentrations of minority ethnic groups had greatly increased in every study area. This reflected partly different Census definitions, but also an actual fairly sharp increase in second generation minority ethnic households, a natural demographic trend resulting from earlier migrations and their age and birth rate profiles. In twelve study areas they had doubled or more as a proportion of the total population (lower panel of Figure 13). By 1991, on average, 19 per cent of the 18 local authorities' population belonged to minority ethnic groups.

On the estates, a twin process was at work. In local authorities with low minority ethnic concentrations, estate populations were more 'white' than the wider local authority. This applied to eight estates in 1981; only one was in London, six were cottage estates in the Midlands and the North, one was a Northern estate of flats. On nine other estates, the concentrations of non-white minority ethnic groups in 1981 were *twice* the local authority average.

By 1991, this process had accelerated, as Figure 13 shows (with estates ordered by minority ethnic population in 1981). The cottage estates with very few minority ethnic households still had virtually none, even though in three of the local authorities the minority ethnic population had grown significantly. The low concentration of minority ethnic groups on certain estates also reflected the location of the cottage estates, far from the original settlement areas of Commonwealth immigrants. However, immigrant newcomers, particularly non-white

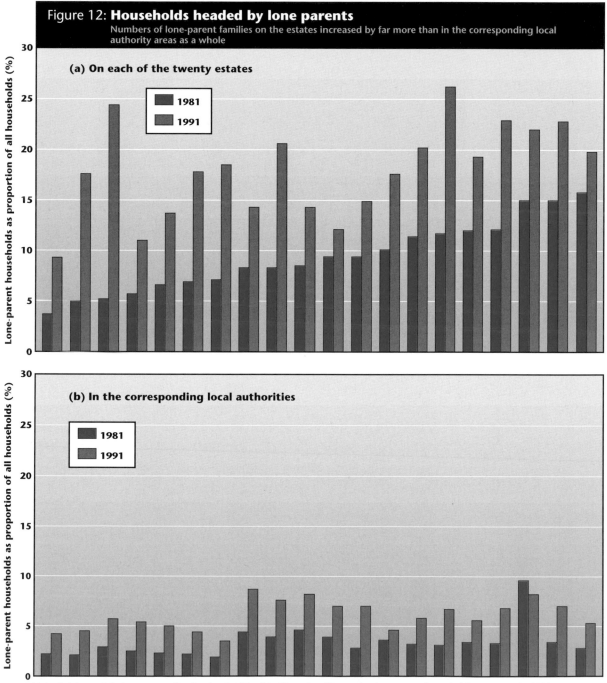

Figure 12: **Households headed by lone parents**
Numbers of lone-parent families on the estates increased by far more than in the corresponding local authority areas as a whole

(a) On each of the twenty estates

(b) In the corresponding local authorities

Note: Estates and their corresponding local authorities listed in order of increasing lone-parent households on estates in 1981.
Source: Census 1981 and 1991.

groups, were still concentrated in older inner city property in these areas, and strong hostility to these newcomers was expressed in some estates in high unemployment areas that were traditionally all-white.

The 12 estates in areas of high minority ethnic concentration all had far above average proportions of minority ethnic households, and the process of concentration had intensified significantly over the 1980s. On seven estates, 45 per cent or more of the population was black.

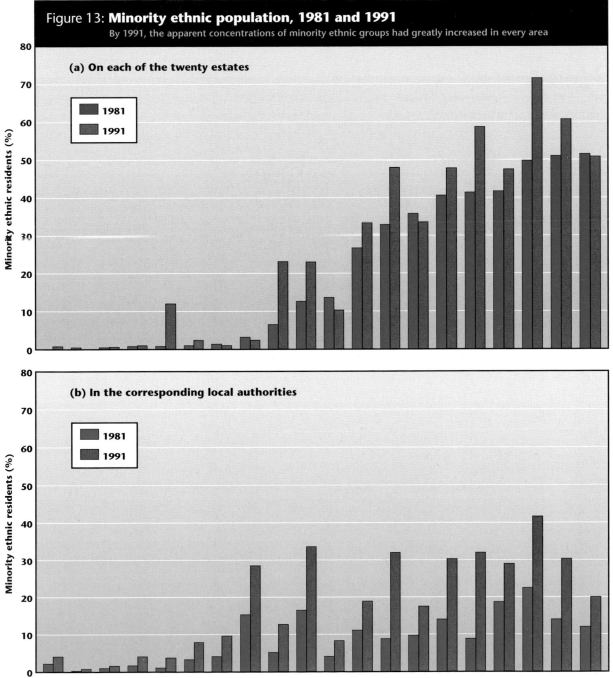

Figure 13: **Minority ethnic population, 1981 and 1991**
By 1991, the apparent concentrations of minority ethnic groups had greatly increased in every area

(a) On each of the twenty estates

1981
1991

Minority ethnic residents (%)

(b) In the corresponding local authorities

1981
1991

Minority ethnic residents (%)

Note: 1981 figures are for proportion of residents in households with a head born in the new Commonwealth or Pakistan.
1991 figures are for respondents' assessment of household members' ethnicity.
Source: Census 1981 and 1991.

On ten estates the concentration was at least 10 per cent above the local authority average. On three estates, three in five of the population were black or belonged to other non-white minorities.

These findings are of great significance. First, since the estates are difficult to manage and generally unpopular, it means that ethnic minorities are disproportionately concentrated in less desirable property, a trend that has been uncovered many times, but is clearly still happening. Second, demand for social housing from minority ethnic groups is probably higher than from the (generally) better housed white population. This tends to reinforce concentrations in less popular areas, particularly through homelessness rehousing routes.[30] Third, once significant concentrations of minority ethnic groups are housed on particular estates, those concentrations seem to intensify. This leads to a barrier developing which white households are reluctant to cross.

Present patterns and trends suggest that minority ethnic concentrations will continue to grow in areas of already high concentration and of high need. This could have implications for urban development that are not yet publicly acknowledged. The impact of minority ethnic communities on urban areas is significant. They often experience higher unemployment levels, have lower incomes and larger families, and experience many forms of discrimination.[31] These factors have combined to make many of the estates, particularly in London, far poorer in 1991 than in 1981, and far poorer than the surrounding areas. The concentration of black people in areas of high disadvantage handicaps them even further, reinforcing the stigma associated with race and forcing black people into the most unpopular estates. This process, first officially detected in 1976,[32] has clearly continued and, if anything, accelerated.

The concentration of minority ethnic groups in these estates had great bearing on the policies adopted towards the estates by local authorities and central government. Additional targeted resources may help redress some of the imbalance created by their population structure.

Some London boroughs had undergone such rapid population change over the 1980s that radical new measures might be justified, both to counter the impact of discrimination and to reverse racial polarisation. Based on our survey, Brent, Lambeth, Lewisham, Hackney, and Haringey experienced the most significant changes, with around 30 per cent or more of their populations now non-white. (Leicester is the only out-of-London authority with a comparable level and rapid rate of increase.) These changes appear to be largely ignored at national level, but raise important questions around issues of equality, discrimination and *the possible emergence of racial ghettos*.

The effect of the population trends on the performance and quality of services requires separate and careful examination.

Educational performance

All schools now publish their GCSE, A level and vocational qualification results. They also publish pupil absentee rates. These published 'league tables' are crude measures of performance, since they do not take into consideration prevailing social and economic conditions. Nor do they necessarily reflect the relative contribution schools make in relation to these conditions. They do, however, show whether children attending certain schools leave with a greater handicap as a result of lower educational achievement.

We identified the secondary schools nearest to the estates with a mixed intake of boys and girls and serving many of the estate children. Where there were no mixed schools (in two estates) we averaged the performance of the nearest boys' and girls' schools (to avoid distortions resulting from the higher performance of girls). We were able to do this, through information gathered during visits, for 16 estates. We then identified the schools in the published league tables for 1994, and compared their performance with the local authority areas and the national average.

We found a consistent gap in exam results between the schools serving the estates and the local authority area schools in general, with an even larger gap between the local authorities and the national average. The schools in these local authorities generally did worse than average, but the estate schools did *even worse*.

There are as yet no generally available tables for primary school performance. These would help clarify how early the educational gap begins. It is likely to start at primary school age, but we do not have firm evidence.

Figure 14 compares the performance of schools serving the estates, the local authorities and nationally by different measures of success at GCSE. The most important finding may be that while 5.5 per cent within the local authorities achieve no GCSEs at any grade, *23 per cent of children in estate-linked schools achieve no GCSEs at any grade*. At the other end of the scale, only 20 per cent (under half the national level) of children attending estate-linked schools achieve five or more GCSEs grades A to C.

These figures reflect the *average* performance of estate-linked secondary schools rather than the achievements of estate children, some of whom attend other schools.

Several other figures reinforce the finding, including A level scores. Only nine of the estate-linked schools offered A levels. Their average score, for pupils taking two or more A levels, was also significantly below the local authority or national average (Figure 15).

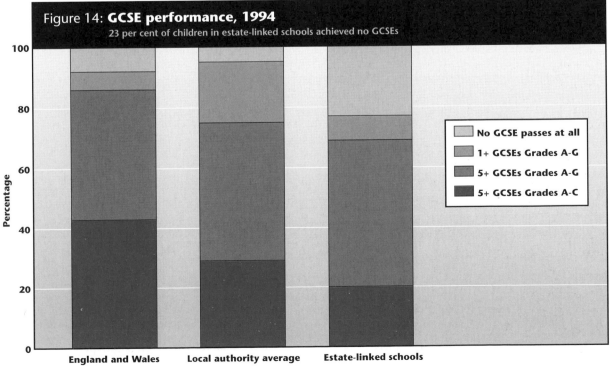

Figure 14: **GCSE performance, 1994**
23 per cent of children in estate-linked schools achieved no GCSEs

Legend:
- No GCSE passes at all
- 1+ GCSEs Grades A-G
- 5+ GCSEs Grades A-G
- 5+ GCSEs Grades A-C

England and Wales   Local authority average   Estate-linked schools

Note: Examinations taken by students who were 15 in September 1993.
Source: Published examination results 1994.

While giving a broad indication of the gap in achievement, the A level figures may be distorted, to a greater extent than GCSE results, by several factors – the existence of sixth form colleges and other further education centres offering A levels, the fact that only nine out of the sixteen estate-linked schools studied offer A levels, and the growth in other post-16 qualifications about which we were able to uncover very little.

Despite these limitations, the figures reveal *a generally poor A level performance* within the 18 local authorities and *a significantly worse performance* in the estate-linked schools, again giving a result *half the national average.*

Truancy

Authorised and unauthorised absence from school has an impact on learning and reflects both parental and pupil attitudes. Authorised absences within the local authorities were close to the national average, but they were significantly higher for the estate-linked schools.

Unauthorised absences, or truanting, were *four times higher* for the estate-linked schools than the national average. For any morning or afternoon session in each of those schools, between 30 and 60 pupils were recorded as truanting. Altogether, at any one time, 16 per cent or *one in six pupils was absent* – in the local authorities one in 10, nationally one in 11 (Figure 16).

This pattern of truancy was related more than circumstantially to the final educational outcome for these pupils. It was another chain of cause and effect, with poor results depressing teacher and pupil expectations, lowering morale and performance, leading to loss of educational motivation, creating a sense of failure, and a desire to abscond.

Vocational training

One way of compensating for these educational problems is to *enhance vocational training and qualifications.* Almost all pupils entered for vocational qualifications achieve them. This

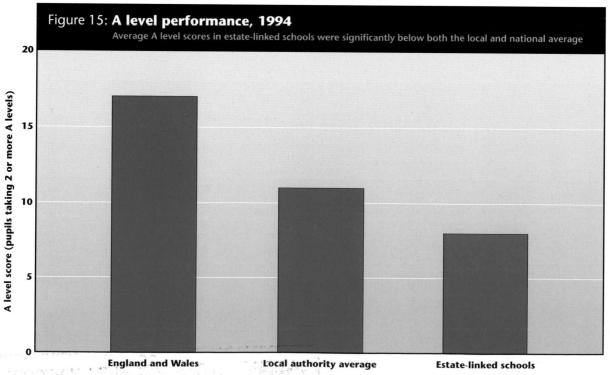

Figure 15: **A level performance, 1994**

Average A level scores in estate-linked schools were significantly below both the local and national average

Note: A level scores based on 2 points for Grade E, 4 points for Grade D, etc. (with half these for AS levels).
Source: Published school examination results 1994.

arguably debases the currency and reflects little more than pupil attendance.

However, vocational qualifications have more relevance than that. First, the skills they represent, though basic, are none the less acquired by the pupils completing them; second, they give the pupils involved a motive for staying at school; third, they form a building block towards further qualifications that can be built on; fourth, if well taught, they can be linked to future work, certainly more easily than truancy or no qualifications at all.

Only seven of the estate-linked schools and only twelve of the local authorities entered pupils for vocational qualifications.

Without further investigation it is impossible to establish the role of vocational qualifications in schools, the potential for expansion and the possible effect on pupil and teacher attitudes. It appeared, however, to be a route forward that

offered some promise of changing attitudes among pupils who were otherwise bound for academic failure.

Tenure change

Local authority renting has been associated with low incomes since 1930, when subsidies for council building were first tied directly to slum clearance. Subsequently, subsidies were additionally tied to relieving overcrowding and rehousing large families in flats and inner city sites, thereby creating a distinctive style and scale of council house building.

Renewed slum clearance programmes in the 1950s and 1960s included special funding for high-rise building. Council rehousing in towns and cities between 1955 and 1975 was almost entirely tied to slum clearance. Over two million crowded and poor quality homes were demolished and around four million families were moved from the poorest inner city areas into council housing.[33] From 1977, the homeless rehousing law required local

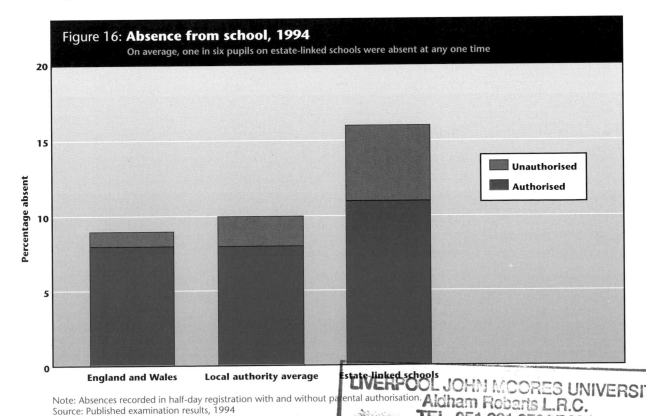

Figure 16: **Absence from school, 1994**

On average, one in six pupils on estate-linked schools were absent at any one time

Note: Absences recorded in half-day registration with and without parental authorisation.
Source: Published examination results, 1994

authorities to give overriding preference to those in priority need and threatened with homelessness.

These evolving programmes and policies meant that council housing in cities and towns, where slums and homelessness were major problems, became more polarised as it grew. Within the council sector, a twin process was at work. Big city and urban authorities built on a large scale with a high proportion of flats, rehousing more slum clearance and homeless cases; smaller, less urban authorities built almost exclusively houses for waiting list applicants in much smaller and less conspicuous settlements.

The least popular housing areas or estates tended to go to the least stable households in a strongly graded rehousing process.[34] Because of these pressures, tenure became associated with economic and social polarisation; and the most difficult to let estates epitomised the extremes of this process.

Owner-occupation was generally a more popular form of tenure, attracting a broad band of people in work, supported by strong government subsidies. Many council tenants, as several surveys showed,[35] aspired to buy but needed more financial help to do so. Over 30 per cent of the country's housing stock, however, was inflexibly tied up in council ownership.

Politicians of both parties had encouraged the sale of council housing and the subsidisation of owner-occupation to meet these aspirations. In 1979, the Conservative Government's radical electoral proposal to introduce the Right to Buy for virtually all council tenants, and for some housing association tenants (it was blocked for charitable associations) broke the mould of property ownership. It offered council tenants the opportunity to purchase an undreamt-of asset at remarkable discounts, if they were in a property they wanted and could cover the often much-

reduced costs. One-quarter of the council stock was sold between 1980 and 1994.

The Right to Buy has had a dramatic impact on the council stock, on the tenure pattern, and on attitudes to renting. But the effect has been uneven (Appendix Table A8).

In the 18 urban local authorities of our study, owner-occupation was traditionally lower than average, and grew more slowly but nonetheless significantly. The council sector was traditionally larger than average and shrunk far more slowly. Nonetheless, about 19 per cent of the council stock (compared with nearly 26 per cent nationally) was sold under Right to Buy by 1994. Private renting was more important in the urban authorities than nationally, but it continued to shrink everywhere. Housing associations grew within the 18 local authorities but still provided only a small minority of rented housing. Overall the tenure shift in the 18 local authorities followed the national pattern but the split between owning and renting was 50/50, whereas for the country as a whole the split was two-thirds/one-third.

On the 20 estates a very different pattern prevailed. In 1980, the estates had been virtually 100 per cent council owned. Between 1981 and 1991, Right to Buy ownership rose from 1 to 5 per cent on average, so levels of owner-occupation remained negligible in most estates. Four estates had some housing association and private developments. Several estates had some demolition, though that did not of itself change the tenure of the estates; the vast majority remained in council ownership. Figure 17 compares the tenure change between 1981 and 1991, in the UK as a whole, in the 18 local authorities, and on the estates.

Figure 18 shows the changed patterns of ownership on the estates by type of estate. The modern estates had the least ownership change.

Resale of flat bought under the 'Right to Buy' scheme, London.

Tenants of new housing association homes built on the site of demolished blocks, North London.

"*The material environment has improved but socio-economic conditions have got worse. Only a change in the economic and employment situation could make for any real and major improvements in conditions on the estate.*"
Resident

The balcony flats surprisingly had the most Right to Buy, probably owing to higher discounts combined with more popular locations (inner city, older areas) and more jobs. On 18 of the 20 estates sales were well below half the average. On 13 estates, less than 5 per cent was sold.

Figure 19 shows graphically the dominance of council ownership, the small inroads made by the Right to Buy in most estates and the impact of demolition, housing associations and developers in seven estates.

The overwhelming dominance of council ownership at the end of a period of intense government activity to encourage tenure diversity, privatisation, and owner-occupation confirmed and reflected the social composition of the estates.[36] The limited tenure change reinforced the highly segregated character of most of the estates and the difficulty in breaking up council

ownership without more radical measures in unpopular areas. By 1994, two estates, the two furthest to the right in Figure 19, had been partially transformed through radical demolition, disposal and expensive renewal; plans were advanced to transform at least five other estates through more or less radical renewal programmes usually involving substantial transfer of ownership. We will discuss these changes in more detail below.

To the extent that the estates were still overwhelmingly council-owned, the concentrations of need within them appeared almost inevitable. A crucial question therefore was the extent to which the population and tenure polarisation prevented or limited progress. We examine this in the next chapter.

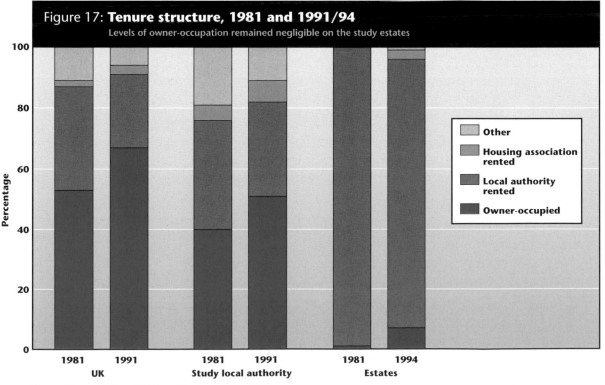

Figure 17: Tenure structure, 1981 and 1991/94

Levels of owner-occupation remained negligible on the study estates

Legend:
- Other
- Housing association rented
- Local authority rented
- Owner-occupied

UK: 1981, 1991
Study local authority: 1981, 1991
Estates: 1981, 1994

Source: Census 1981 and 1991 and local managers, 1994.

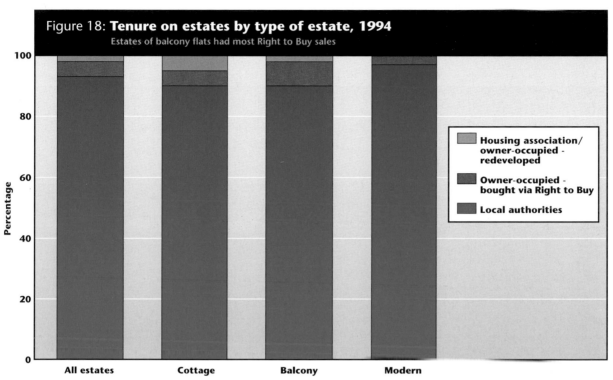

Figure 18: **Tenure on estates by type of estate, 1994**
Estates of balcony flats had most Right to Buy sales

Legend:
- Housing association/ owner-occupied - redeveloped
- Owner-occupied - bought via Right to Buy
- Local authorities

Note: All stock was local authority tenure in 1980.
Source: Local and senior managers.

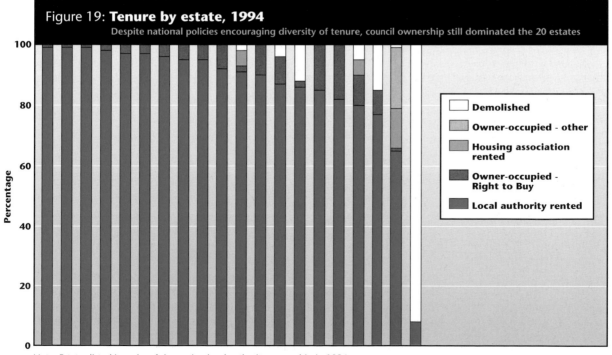

Figure 19: **Tenure by estate, 1994**
Despite national policies encouraging diversity of tenure, council ownership still dominated the 20 estates

Legend:
- Demolished
- Owner-occupied - other
- Housing association rented
- Owner-occupied - Right to Buy
- Local authority rented

Note: Estates listed in order of decreasing local authority ownership in 1994.
Source: Local and senior managers

5

Progress on estates: the evidence

This chapter provides detailed evidence based on the visits and drawn from discussions with staff and residents. Wherever possible, we compare what we found in 1994 with the situation in 1988, 1982 and 1979-80.

Original problems

Before local housing management began, the estates had:

- poor physical conditions, disrepair and environmental decay;
- management problems with high arrears, high turnover and difficulty in letting property;
- large numbers of children and young people;
- an isolated or unfavourable location;
- a concentration of people with social and economic problems.

There were many reasons for the intense decay we encountered. Among the most important were:

- unwieldy and destructive slum clearance programmes between 1930 and 1975 which stigmatised the first occupants of many new council estates;[37]
- very rapid expansion in newly-built council stock over the 1960s and 1970s with insufficient management capacity to handle the growth;
- an almost total lack of ground level services to maintain estate conditions;[38]
- a lack of resident involvement in decisions about their estates, particularly their design,

and resulting alienation from their landlord;
- the scale of estate developments and growing reliance on untried and unconventional design;[39]
- the failure of government to establish a structure for the housing service even remotely comparable with other parts of the welfare state;[40]
- reorganisation of local authorities in 1974 into vast, highly complex landlord organisations with greatly expanded boundaries and a doubling or tripling in size;
- discriminatory rehousing systems in common use, leading to a strong hierarchy of estates.[41]

The start of estate-based management

By 1979 the least popular estates were extremely vulnerable. Local authority landlords were the first to react, and special projects had begun by 1982 on these 20 estates. Four were started before 1979 (one before 1978), when the Government first directly supported local management initiatives, and a further four in 1979. The majority were set up from 1980 onwards – six in 1980 and seven in 1981 (see Appendix Table A2).

Estate-based management was not a new idea. It dated from the Victorian era when Octavia Hill reformed slum conditions through assiduous attention to tenant relations and a passion for detail. Her crusading style evolved into tight management control. It was emulated by Philanthropic Trusts, like Peabody, but it could not easily be adopted by local

Major internal works, North East.

Removal of overhead walkways and recladding of blocks through Estate Action, London.

"The capital works programme was very important as a tangible improvement for tenants, and enabled the tenants' association to get off the ground." Local manager

authorities with their diffuse multi-purpose bureaucracies and political accountability.[42]

The estate initiatives of the late 1970s and early 1980s were premised on establishing an estate base because of the breakdown in control and communication.[43] The logic of 'hands-on' management, local control and tenant involvement flowed readily from the estate base. In the authority vacuum hanging over estates and the morass of neglect and need that had grown up, immediate action to stem the decay flowed readily and quickly. Local offices immediately engaged in change on many fronts; the broader the base for tackling problems, the more likely was the project to succeed, the stronger the base of support among residents, and the greater the overall impact.

The changes on the estates stemming from the introduction of estate initiatives fell into three main categories: physical reinvestment; local management of ground-level conditions; social initiatives and tenant involvement.

Physical reinvestment
Unchangeable aspects
Estate location and basic design were of course immutable. They combined to create continuing problems for all, bar three, estates. One smaller cottage estate, close to the centre of town, is now well-modernised, stable and popular. One small balcony estate was likewise well-located and reasonably successfully modernised. One large northern modern estate had never been fully occupied, became obsolete and was almost completely demolished, save three popular blocks, close together, which have been

Table 4: **Capital works, 1988–94, on 20 estates**	
Physical measures taken to tackle problems on estates	Number of estates
Upgrading dwelling fabric	
windows	11
roofs	11
internal (including central heating)	10
walls (insulation, crumbling concrete, damp, etc.)	7
Environment	
roads and parking	12
landscaping	8
communal services, e.g. drains	7
play	4
Security	
doors and window locks strengthening	17
extra lighting	14
fencing	12
door controls	12
• with video camera controls	4
• with concierge	6
strengthened glass	8
walkway and bridge removal	5
Total number of estates with dwelling and environmental upgrading	19
Total number of estates with some security measures	19
Source: Local managers and residents.	

successfully and expensively renovated. These three estates are *not* adversely affected by location and design. The other 17 estates have continuing problems. Scale, uniformity and public character interact to make them at best conspicuously separate from normal streets, at worst ugly and oppressive in appearance. This has *not* changed.

There were therefore severe limits to the possible impact of physical works. Nonetheless they were popular with residents and staff; were a prerequisite for eliminating some of the most difficult management problems; and made the estates more attractive even if failing to eradicate the most fundamental problems.

Upgrading

Nineteen of the 20 estates have had some physical upgrading since 1988, including buildings, environment and security. Table 4 shows the range of capital works and number of estates undergoing each type. Appendix Table A5 shows funding sources.

Modern complex estates underwent the greatest amount of capital work covering the most elements (see Table 5). In particular, security was a much bigger problem on the modern

Table 5: **Average number of physical measures taken to tackle problems by type of estate, 1988–94**			
Type of estate	Dwellings and environment	Security	Total
cottage	3	5	8
balcony	4	5	9
modern	5	8	13

Source: Local managers and residents.

estates and many more measures were tried to counter design problems.

The amount of money spent per estate (1988 to 1994) ranged from only £25 to £50,000 per unit. We divided costs to date per estate by the total units on that estate as the simplest way of showing the effect on the *whole* estate, even though works were sometimes only carried out to part of them. Six estates were in the middle of major programmes with extremely costly additional works still planned in 1994. We identified these future costs separately. No figures were available for two estates. Table 6 shows the average costs to date by type of estate, varying from an average under £1,000 on balcony estates to over £12,000 on modern estates.

Table 6: **Average cost per unit of capital works, 1988–94**	
	Average cost per unit (£)
Works to date (figures from 18 estates)	
cottage	3,287
balcony	728
modern	12,720
Planned works (affecting 5 estates)	
total restructuring of existing estates (3 estates)	31,000
substantial demolition and block transformation (1 estate)	50,000
total demolition and rebuilding (1 estate)	85,000

Note: Planned works affected northern and London estates. The high unit cost of planned works reflects only estimated contract prices and does not allow for the cost of any net loss of units.
Source: Local managers

Estate restructuring

"We want streets with houses on them, not an estate." Resident, modern estate, London

Five estates were embarking on or in the middle of work that fundamentally altered the design of the estates. This work was of a different order of magnitude, as Table 6 shows. These costs of full replacement and of major restructuring are so high as to be prohibitive except in a very few instances. The costs where demolition took place usually *do not allow for net loss of units.* Fewer units will be replaced after demolition, due to the shortage of land and high cost. In areas shortage of land and of low demand, loss of units is a major justification for demolition. In areas of high demand, this loss is a major additional cost. The demolition option is usually unviable *as long as there is housing need and demand*, unless the estate is unsaveable. The extremely high cost of either restructuring or of demolition and replacement made a more incremental, lower level approach inevitable in most places.

Assessment of capital works

"People sit out and talk to each other and spend a lot of money on their new gardens, which benefits everyone – this is directly related to the improvement work." Local manager

Residents' and managers' views of the works to date are shown in Table 7. Mixed outcomes implied some success, but some elements not working satisfactorily. More problems arose on modern estates than on other types of estate, though all encountered some. Door controls and concierge systems were the *most* prone to failure. But poor tenant liaison, poor programming and poor management of works were problems in two cases. Modern estates were inevitably the most difficult because of their complex physical structure and design. Managers' assessments of outcomes were generally more positive than residents'. In four-fifths of the estates, they believed the improvements were successful. Residents rated the capital works successful in half the estates, in many cases saying the results were mixed. In only two estates did residents assess capital works as *unsuccessful.*

Table 7: **Managers' and residents' assessment of capital works, 1988-94**

	Successful	Mixed	Unsuccessful	NA/DK
Local managers' assessment				
all estates	14	4	0	2[1]
cottage	5	0	0	2
balcony	5	1	0	0
modern	4	3	0	0
Residents' assessment				
all estates	7	5	2	2[1]
cottage	3	1	1	1
balcony	1	2[2]	0	1
modern	3	2	1	0

Notes: Residents' views were not collected on three estates.
1 In one estate almost no work has been done; in another work is ongoing and the manager could not express an opinion.
2 This reflected the inadequate *level* of spending rather than problems with the works themselves.

Housing management change

"Last year there was a long, hot summer – noise, drinking, people sitting out on the steps. The manager could calm it down by her mere presence." Resident

"They still do everything as if they're doing you a big favour ... they're rude in the extreme. They don't have to live here, they're going home to nice, cushy houses ... They lack motivation, they have a poor attitude." Resident

"Staff are so responsive, beyond job descriptions and normal expectations." Local manager

"I love being estate-based and having that kind of involvement." Local manager

Since 1980–81, when all the estates had a local office, certain basic features of local housing management have been central to success:

- a permanent estate base open most of the time to tenants;
- locally-based, full-time staff with estate officers covering small patches or areas;
- major responsibility for housing management services devolved to the local offices;
- close links with residents.

Two of the 20 offices have closed. The rest have continued to operate on these basic principles. The management changes between 1981 and 1994 have been evolutionary and incremental. Offices now have *more responsibility* than in 1981 (Figure 20) and have more specialised staff, such as housing benefit staff (Figure 21). Local budgets are now in place in 12 offices (Table 8), although only two offices have full local budgets.

However, offices now cover almost *twice the number of units* than in 1981 (Table 9). Apart from one case, offices have remained on the

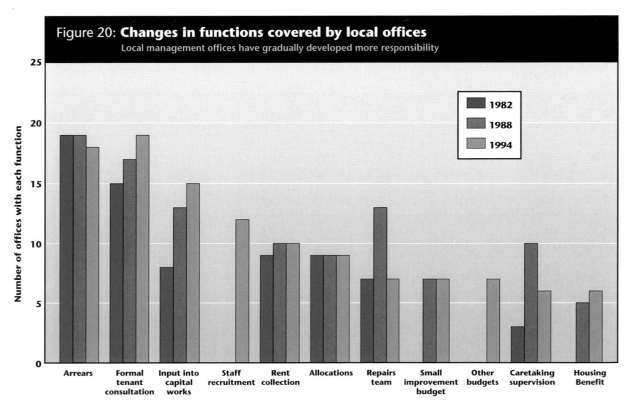

Figure 20: **Changes in functions covered by local offices**
Local management offices have gradually developed more responsibility

same estates. The change in area size has also been incremental, involving repeated reorganisation within local authorities. The ratio of staff to properties increased dramatically at the outset of the projects. As functions moved to the estates, the ratio improved further (Table 10). Over the last few years, staff ratios have dropped slightly, but they are still at least double the pre-project levels.

Opening

From the outset the majority of offices have opened all day, four to five days a week. In 1994, staff were available to see tenants throughout most of the day in 15 offices. The number of callers per week ranged from 80 to 800. It did not depend on the size or type of estate, though in general cottage estate offices had more callers (Figure 22). It appeared to vary with the quality of service, the range of functions the staff controlled and the availability of staff.

Empty property

"Two years ago there were huge numbers of voids – cul de sacs that were just terrible – and hundreds of requests for transfers off."
Local manager

Table 8: **Number of estates with budgets**

Type of budget	1982	1988	1994
Small improvement budget only	0	7	5
repairs budget only	0	0	1
staff and office costs only	0	0	4
repairs, staff and office costs	0	0	2
total estates with local budgets	0	7	12

Source: Local and senior managers

Table 9: **Average number of homes covered by local offices**

Type of estate	Number of units managed by local office		
	1982	1988	1994
all estates	1,062	1,557	1,877
cottage	900	1,473	1,343
balcony	949	1,793	2,745
modern	1,321	1,473	1,688

Source: Local managers

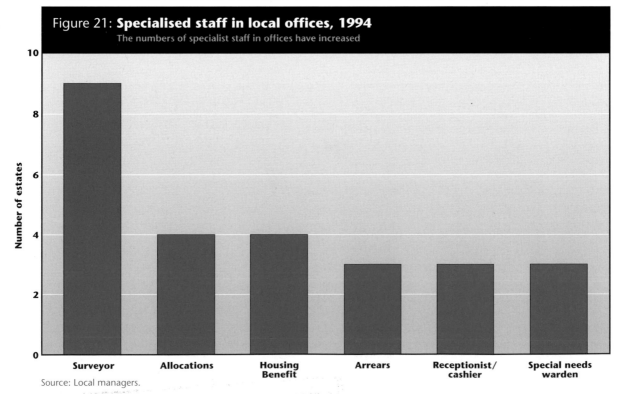

Figure 21: **Specialised staff in local offices, 1994**
The numbers of specialist staff in offices have increased

Source: Local managers.

The level of empty property has been a clear barometer of problems from the outset. Over the period of local management, void levels have fallen. Lettings crises on seven estates over the 1980s affected modern and cottage estates more than balcony estates. Table 11 shows the trend overall and on 13 estates which did not experience acute lettings crises.

The overall picture disguises some important differences between estates. While a majority of estates have had less than 5 per cent of their property empty since the estate projects began, a significant minority with extreme lettings problems at different times over the 1980s had much higher levels, in two cases with 50 per cent of the homes empty. Figure 23 shows the speed at which voids grew in these crisis estates.

Table 10: **Ratio of properties to staff**

Type of estate	Housing officers' patch size		
	1982	1988	1994
all estates	**447**	**344**	**364[1]**
cottage	**454**	**387**	**351**
balcony	**586**	**340**	**393[1]**
modern	**428**	**304**	**357**

Note: 1 One balcony estate with exceptional patch size – 789 – is excluded; if included, the average for balcony is 459 and average for all estates is 386.

Source: Local managers

Table 11: **Empty properties 1980–94**

	Percentage of total stock empty			
	Start of project	1982	1988	1994
Average of 17 estates for which complete figures are available	**6.5**	**5.7**	**7.9**	**4.4**
Average of 13 estates that have not had lettings crises	**5.1**	**2.6**	**2.8**	**3.3**

Source: Local managers

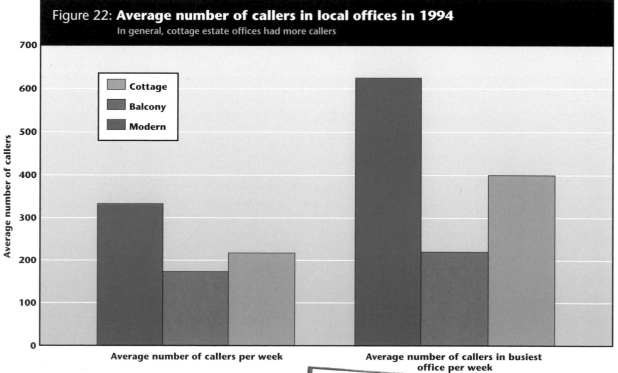

Figure 22: **Average number of callers in local offices in 1994**
In general, cottage estate offices had more callers

Legend: Cottage, Balcony, Modern

Y-axis: Average number of callers

Average number of callers per week

Average number of callers in busiest office per week

Source: Local managers.

Housing officer and resident in consultation, North West.

Empty home, North East.

"We have voids, and we have homeless people in hostels, but it's not as simple as that. We have to choose people who are going to make a contribution to the estate. There isn't much other investment here – we need to invest in human resources." Assistant director

From the outset of local management, local administration of letting has led to lower levels of empty property and greater success in letting property in nearly half the estates. In depopulating regions this approach has been uncontroversial. In London it has been much more difficult to implement, even where there is too little demand to fill particular estates. But our surveys have consistently shown over 15 years that centralised lettings to unpopular estates, even in areas of high demand, lead to *more empty* property. Localised lettings, even where demand is low, lead to *less empty* property (Figure 24).

Under pressure to rehouse homeless families, many London authorities introduced a policy of 'one offer only' for homeless families in the late 1980s, meaning that they had to accept vacancies wherever they were available, usually on unpopular estates. This strongly centralised policy was too insensitive and inflexible, allowing no local input or connection. It provoked more refusals than a more locally sensitive approach and therefore had a direct impact on the level of empty units, pushing up the numbers of voids on some large London estates. Figure 25 shows the contrasting development of voids before and after such policies were introduced.

Lettings are highly susceptible to changes in management and policy. Local or central control of lettings administration emerged as a dominant feature in controlling estate conditions.

Turnover

Turnover was still higher than the local authority average on most estates, even though it had fallen from the extraordinarily high levels prevailing on most estates before the local projects began. Estates in crisis can have up to 40 per cent turnover a year. Table 12 shows the changing pattern of turnover. No estate now has more than 20 per cent of tenants leaving a

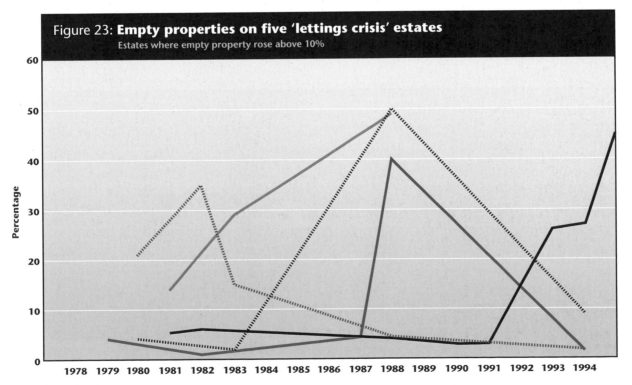

Figure 23: **Empty properties on five 'lettings crisis' estates**
Estates where empty property rose above 10%

1978 1979 1980 1981 1982 1983 1984 1985 1986 1987 1988 1989 1990 1991 1992 1993 1994

Source: Local managers.

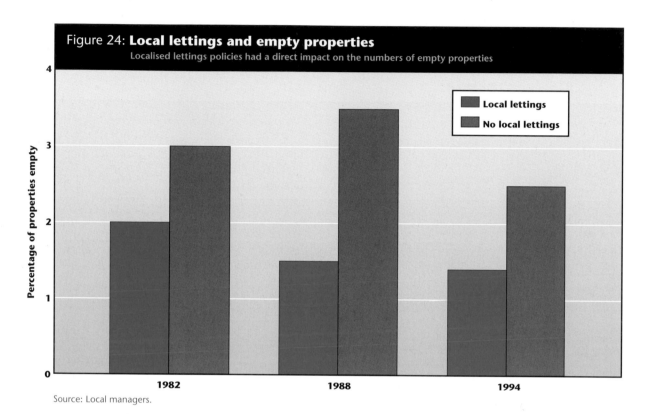

Source: Local managers.

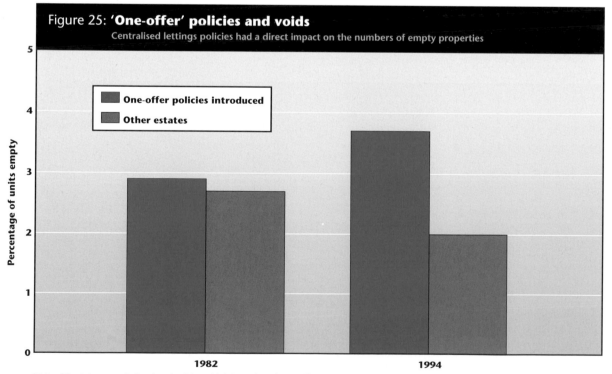

Note: 10 estates were in local authorities which introduced one-offer policies in mid-1980s. 5 estates with lettings crises are excluded as they were all estates in extreme low demand regions.
Source: Local managers.

year, although many still have over 10 per cent – more than double the local authority level in most cases. This reflects quite a high level of instability, almost certainly linked to the disproportionately high unemployment rates and youthful character of the population.

Table 12: **Turnover of estate population 1982–94**

	Number of estates		
% per year	1982	1988	1994
under 10	2	10	7
10–20	7	2	8
over 20	5	4	0
all	14	16	15

Note: Only includes estates with figures available
Source: Local managers.

Table 13: **Average rent levels in the local authorities with the 20 estates, 1982–94**

	Rent for 2-bed property (£ per week)		
	1982	1988	1994
all estates	26	38	40
cottage	22.50	na	29
balcony	25	na	44
modern	32.50	na	50

Source: Local managers.

Arrears

"Staff have improved their performance, because it is what we collect that will mean we can deliver a service —we know there's no extra money for the Housing Revenue Account." Local manager

"The managers work with tenants. They don't let you run up £1,000 arrears." Resident

Between 1982 and 1994, rent levels rose by over 50 per cent (Table 13) whereas arrears rose by 77 per cent on the 20 estates. Rent and arrears levels vary widely by region and type of estate. We calculated arrears both in cash, and in weeks of rent owing to control for varied and rising rents (Table 14). On cottage estates, arrears – historically low – have reduced slightly. Balcony estates now have much the same average level of arrears in weeks owing as in 1980. Modern estates have had higher average arrears throughout the study period, and they rose rapidly in cash and weeks owing, but this was almost entirely explained by a single estate where arrears tripled over the period. The arrears crisis on this estate has now been contained. Arrears on the modern estates fell by almost 24 per cent between 1993 and 1994, with the advent of ring-fencing, performance monitoring and Compulsory Competitive Tendering accelerating

Table 14: **Rent arrears, 1982–94**

	Total arrears per tenant, £ (number of weeks owing in brackets)			
	1982	1988	1993	1994
all estates	146 (6)	164 (4)	310 (8)	258 (6)
cottage	94 (4)	92 (na)	103 (4)	77 (3)
balcony	120 (5)	184 (na)	217 (5)	275 (6)
modern	195 (6)	335 (na)	634 (13)	483 (10)

Note: Two estates with full figures not available are excluded.
Source: Local managers and local authorities.

the introduction of cost centres and local budgeting. It is clear that rent income now directly influences local managers' scope for spending.

Overall, arrears are now falling quite steeply in cash. In weeks owing they are back down to 1980 levels, but remain a continuing problem.

Housing benefit

Of the 18 estates with complete rent information, seven had localised housing benefit administration, most since the late 1980s. Five of the seven offices were on London estates, covering large areas, with traditionally high arrears. We compared the arrears performance of offices with and without localised housing benefit administration by region (London and outside). With localised benefit service, arrears were significantly lower both inside and outside London (Table 15). For all the estates together, arrears were higher on the estates with local housing benefit administration, but this was purely a composition effect reflecting the greater proportion of London estates where this was in place.

Caretaking and cleaning

"The estate is cleaner now than ever before, better managed and better repaired. It helps to have a local office – but you need a competitive environment, and an administration that will be brutal if necessary... CCT provided a tool for this restructuring." Tenant participation worker

"One of the caretakers was fighting in Bosnia when he was supposed to be working on this estate... I saw someone peeing in that stairwell – it was the surveyor!" Resident

There were several important changes in the way caretaking and cleaning services were organised. The role of caretaker and cleaner had been combined on 11 estates. At the same time, caretakers were now more commonly expected to do some minor repairs as part of their jobs. Caretaking had increased and was now more common on cottage estates as well as estates of flats. But it had been improved by competitive tendering. It was more tightly structured, more carefully specified and more controlled. Housing managers felt that contracting for cleaning, environmental and custodial services had greatly helped.

Concierges had become popular on the modern estates. Concierge systems on five of the seven modern estates involved permanent custodial staff being placed at a reception desk in the entrances of tower blocks to control and personalise access, to

---

Table 15: Impact of localised housing benefit service on arrears performance, 1994 (average number of weeks' rent owing)

	All estates	London estates	Other estates
Estates with local housing benefit administration:			
weeks owing	6.4	6.8	2.0
number of estates	7	5	2
Estates without local housing benefit administration:			
weeks owing	5.5	9.9	2.9
number of estates	11	4	7
Average arrears for all estates (weeks)	5.9	8.2	2.7

Note: Two estates without complete information are excluded.
Source: Estimates based on information from local authorities.

Door security, London.

"It's a sad thing that eight or ten people could cause such havoc on the estate. One or two will always be in and out of prison, but if you catch them, the people they attract will grow out of it." Resident

report on any difficulties and to maintain block conditions. However, they did not work as hoped on several estates because the staff employed as concierges often had little training or back-up, too limited job descriptions, and too little to do.

Estate patrols have become popular on over half the estates, although surprisingly most of the modern estates, which would seem to need them, do not have them.

Overall there were far fewer complaints about the standards of caretaking in 1994 than there had been in 1981 or 1987. In several places they were highly praised. Table 16 summarises the structure and impact (on 13 estates) of caretaking services. With only one exception, the impact was improved or the same.

Repairs

> "I would like to address disrepair problems
> of the estate in a more strategic and efficient
> manner, but funding is not available."
> Local manager

The organisation of repairs on the estates changed dramatically over the 1980s (Appendix Table A6).

It went from highly centralised in-house organisations, to localised, more integrated services on the estates, and then to a contract service. The creation of central direct labour organisations as separate contractors after 1982 led to the creation of larger areas but more streamlined structures. Now Compulsory Competitive Tendering for housing management is raising the issue of direct control over repairs contracts by local management contractors. Local managers, as they increasingly gained their own budgets, were beginning to influence repairs standards.

In most areas, direct labour organisations were awarded most contracts, but some work was going to outside contractors. In three authorities, the repairs tail clearly still wagged the housing management dog. This resulted from political pressure to ensure that direct labour organisations retained the lion's share of the contracts. Based on figures from 10 estates, the cost of repairs to the estates - £9.44 - was close to the local authority average - £9.11 (see Appendix Table A7).

In over half the estates, local managers felt that repairs were improving. Residents were more

	Number of estates			
	All	Cottage	Balcony	Modern
caretaker/cleaners	12	2	5	6
cleaners only	4	2	1	
concierges (one discontinued)	5	0	0	5
estate patrols	11	6	4	2
sheltered wardens	3	3	0	0
estates with some custodial services	16	3	6	7

Assessment of caretaking/cleaning, 1988–94 (13 estates)

improved	8
same	4
deteriorated	1

Source: Local managers and residents.

Table 16: Structure and assessment of caretaking service by type of estate, 1994

critical of the repairs service than staff, but they were mainly dissatisfied with the amount of work that was possible and the time it took to do it, compared with what they saw as necessary. Information on repairs was still inadequate, as was the local control of repairs contracts. This was expected to change when housing management contracts were introduced in 1996. Generally, in 1994 the estates were in a far better state of repair and were better maintained than they had been in 1980 or 1987. Most local authorities still do not have planned maintenance.

The cost of localised housing management

The direct costs of local housing management can be justified if conditions and performance improve. The cost of staff inputs into housing management, averaged across the 12 estates for which complete information was available, was £2.87 per unit per week. This figure excludes office costs, central overheads and support services. The overall local authority cost of the full housing management service including all central and local costs was £13.58 per unit per week (Appendix Table A7). The staffing costs for estate-based management thus represented an estimated 21 per cent of the full management cost of the local authority housing service. This proportion of overall costs targeted on particularly vulnerable estates seemed to produce gains in local conditions that we believe outweigh the costs.[44]

Resident involvement and the links with housing management

"When I first came, the staff were worried about the residents' reps, but now they welcome them... it should be joint management, management by agreement. We're dealing with the people that pay our wages. The 'us and them' attitude has completely gone." Local manager

On most estates, tenants were involved in running their own groups, providing services for residents, participating in local management decisions, and lobbying over problems and priorities. By far the biggest change over the fifteen years was the growth in the number of estates where joint liaison meetings and groups between the local staff and residents had been set up with council support. The joint structures were significant in maintaining the flow of information, ideas, and problem-solving. Housing management was far more successful and less problematic as a result.

Half the managers believed that resident initiative and involvement had been crucial to securing capital works. Tenants had often lobbied and argued for spending, even to the Department of the Environment (DoE). Staff felt that this was more powerful than local authority presentations! It was the highest priority for residents, which may help to explain their success. Table 17 shows the frequency of contact between the council and resident groups.

Table 17: **Frequency of meetings between council staff and residents' groups, 1994**	
Frequency	Number of estates
At least:	
fortnightly	**6**
monthly	**8**
less often – on request	**2**
no active group	**4**
Source: Local managers and residents.	

A major development was the emergence of Estate Management Boards, which give tenants a controlling say in how their area is run through a local board with a majority of elected resident representatives, working in partnership with the local authority. The Board is legally

Members of resident-run youth club, London.

Members of indoor bowling club, North East.

"It's like a village when you get settled in. It's really friendly. I love living here." Resident

registered as a company or industrial and provident society and has a formal management agreement with the council, giving it responsibility for some of the council's landlord functions. Although this idea was proposed in ten estates, it only took root in four. The estates with tenant management initiatives and Estate Management Boards had a greater degree of staff autonomy, greater levels of tenant involvement and greater outside support than other estates.

Table 18 summarises the ways residents are organised and involved. Tenants' groups are open to Right to Buy leaseholders and owners. They are often called tenants' *and* residents' associations. In gathering information we counted as tenants' and residents' associations those groups with a formal constitution recognised by the council, and with an agreed role in consulting with local staff and the council over housing management and other estate matters.

Support for tenants' groups

Funding for residents' groups and activities was minimal. They mainly raised their own money through social events and local fund-raising. One-third of groups received a small annual grant (often under £200); another third had received small start-up grants of a few hundred pounds.

Only Estate Management Boards received significant funds under the Government's Section 16 programme – about £35–50,000 over 2½ years, three-quarters from the DoE, a quarter from local authorities. Most of this was paid over by the tenants' groups to agencies who helped with development, training, and negotiation of the management agreement with the local authority.

One of the major forms of support on the survey estates was the local management office, giving the tenants close links with the council. If CCT seriously curtails the role of these offices in relation to tenant involvement, this could have serious consequences for the future role of tenants.

Table 19 shows the way the groups were organised and the support they received. The four Estate Management Boards in 1994 received support under every heading. This was justified by the level of responsibility they were assuming and was made possible by their separate budgets and government funding. It indicated that if tenants were to assume any real degree of power or control, they needed considerably more back-up than most groups actually received.

Six proposed Estate Management Boards had faced serious problems and were unlikely to proceed. On one estate the council had suspended the process due to conflict between

Table 18: **Types and numbers of residents' organisations on estates, 1982–1994**			
Type of organisation	Number of estates with organisations		
	1982	1988	1994
joint council/tenants' advisory group	4	12	16
active tenants'/residents' association	16	13	15
Estate Management Board	0	0	4

Note: One estate management board was in a state of flux at the time of writing.

Table 19: **Support for residents' groups**

	Number of groups			Number of EMBs receiving support
	1982	1988	1994	1994
active groups	16	13	16	4
access to premises	16	13	15	4
regular meetings with housing officers	na	13	17	4
access to councillors	na	na	10	4
local authority funding	na	na	10	4
Department of the Environment funding	na	na	4	4
worker support	17	na	9	4
training for members	0	4	8	4

Source: Local managers and residents.

two rival groups. On another, the Director effectively declared that no additional repairs money would become available and the Board would have to 'make do'. In two, tenants' groups had fallen foul of the council in attempting to pursue the Right to Manage. This policy, giving tenants legal control of their estates, was subject to many complex requirements which often alienated both councils and tenants. It appeared a deterrent to the development of further tenant management organisations.

Problems with tenant involvement

"Difficult to keep people involved in running things; people fell out with each other, the early momentum was lost... terribly sad."
Resident

Activists reported many problems in keeping a wider body of tenants involved. There were many complaints of apathy and some resident leaders showed signs of being battle-worn and disillusioned.

On three estates there were two or more residents' groups. In two there was tension between the older, more traditional residents and younger, more challenging and more active groups. In one case the younger group comprised almost exclusively lone parents.

Table 20 highlights the most common problems facing residents' groups in their internal organisation, from the perspective of managers working with them. Four managers said there were no problems. From the tenants' point of view, problems included lack or shortage of resources, difficulty in being heard, insufficient power, and lack of wider interest among residents. A surprising problem among tenants' leaders was some resentment of workers who were seen to take money and power *away* from residents and who sometimes supplanted the community development work residents were aiming to do.

Local services and facilities

"We need a supermarket – it's like being on a desert island." Resident

The increase in resident involvement had gone hand-in-hand with improved and expanded services and facilities. Community services were generally targeted towards vulnerable age

Young people learning to use computer equipment, London.

Tenant leader.

"They're consulting us more, it's a cultural change.
But they don't take us seriously enough." Resident

Table 20: **Problems facing residents' groups, according to managers, 1994**

Problems	Number of estates
low numbers involved in group	7
unrepresentativeness and limited accountability of those involved	5
insufficient involvement in management and estate problems	4
conflicts between rival groups	2

Source: Local managers.

Table 21: **Activities and services available in the estate**

Number of estates with activities and services	1982	1988	1994
for elderly	10	13	15
for under-fives	11	17	18
for young people	14	12	13
for adult women	na	3	4[1]
for ethnic groups	na	6	5
economic support and self-help, e.g. employment resource centres, credit unions, food co-ops	na	7	10
Total	35	58	65

Note:
1 Also one men's group.
Source: Local managers and residents.

groups and social groups with special needs. Table 21 shows the steady increase in provision and the type of activities that were organised. Half the estates were attempting economic initiatives, in response to money and work problems. Residents participated directly in these activities.

A majority of estates lack many basic facilities, although they may be provided within walking distance. By 1994, most estates had community centres, a few basic shops, nearby bus routes, and nursery provision (Table 22). Inner city estates had the greatest range of facilities within reach (fifteen minutes' walk), but this distance was a problem for families with young children, older, and disabled people. One-third of estates had lost some shops between 1981 and 1994 and prices were high. But shops appeared generally better-run in 1994 than at the outset.

Crime, anti-social behaviour and estate stigma

"I've been burgled eight times." Resident

"It's a sad thing that eight or ten people could cause such havoc on the estate. One or two won't grow out of it and will be always in and out of prison, but if you catch them, the people they attract will grow out of it." Resident

From the outset the 20 estates had serious crime problems. They still do (Table 23). But many problems have been reduced or are being contained through a combination of high spending on security measures, the strong local presence of housing staff, frequent liaison between the police, residents, the local offices, and resident organisations. Social problems which contributed greatly to anti-social

Table 22: **Estate and neighbourhood facilities in 1994**

Number of estates with facilities	In estate	Within 15 minutes' walk
community centre, flat or room available for free communal use	18	20
basic shops, e.g. newsagent, convenience store	13	20
bus route	11	19
nursery	11	17
primary school	8	18
Post Office	5	17
doctor	5	14
clinic	5	12
launderette	5	13
chemist	4	15
secondary school	2	13
train/underground station	0	12
wider range of shops	0	15
supermarket	0	11

Source: Local managers and residents.

Table 23: **Types of crime and anti-social behaviour occurring in estates, 1994**

Crime	Number of estates
vandalism	15
burglary	15
racial harassment	15
drug dealing/use	14
theft of and theft from cars	8
'mugging'	7
general harassment/loitering/delinquency	7
'joyriding'	5

Note: Many estates had more than one problem.
Source: Local managers, and residents.

behaviour, weak control and sometimes breakdown had not got easier. Therefore crime was being tackled in a generally more difficult environment.

The problems most directly relating to crime and anti-social behaviour were: the concentration of unemployed young people; family breakdown; domestic violence; drug and alcohol problems; neighbour disputes and noise nuisance; poor control over children.

Figure 26 gives the views of residents and managers on this problem. Residents on most estates thought crime was a big problem, and none thought it a small problem. Managers were more evenly divided between thinking crime was a small or large problem. All types of estate were affected by crime.

Table 24 shows that in a majority of estates, residents and managers thought crime problems had reduced or at least not got worse over the last six years. In many ways this is the most surprising finding of all, revealing as it does a view that crime problems are being contained in spite of greatly increased polarisation. This is almost certainly the result of the big range of activities and improvements including the greatly increased presence of local services.

Design and crime

The connection between design and crime has been heavily disputed in Britain for over a decade.[45] The evidence from our 20 estates has suggested since 1980 that while estates of flats, in particular modern complex estates, are more difficult to manage and live in than houses, they are not necessarily more crime-ridden than the most polarised cottage estates (Figure 26). Crime appears to relate at least as strongly to letting systems, social composition and strength of local management as it does to design. The assessments presented here in part reflect the role of local management in changing the perception of crime.

Guarding and enforcement

One indication that crime problems can be reduced through housing management presence was the growth in patrols, particularly to guard empty property. Eleven estates now have these (Table 16). Guarding has become recognised as a central ingredient of crime prevention as well as an essential component of effective housing management. The much greater local workforce, local activity, local policing and patrolling combined to create natural surveillance, making the estates appear more stable and less crime-prone for residents and managers than in 1987 or 1982.

Table 24: **Perceptions of change in crime level, 1988–94**

Change in crime level as experienced by managers and residents	Local managers' assessment	Residents' assessment	Combined assessment
decreased	7	8	15
stayed the same	7	5	12
increased	5	4	9

Source: Local managers, and residents.

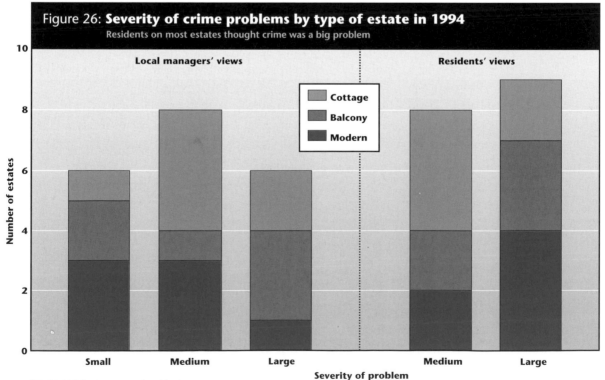

Figure 26: **Severity of crime problems by type of estate in 1994**
Residents on most estates thought crime was a big problem

Source: Local managers and residents.

Table 25: **Changes to tenancy agreements to increase power of enforcement, 1988-94**			
Changes to tenancy agreement	Changes made	Changes planned	No change
all estates	13	4	2
cottage	4	3	0
balcony	3	1	1
modern	6	0	1

Source: Local managers.

Changing tenancy agreements to strengthen enforcement powers had become common as a way of curbing crime and anti-social behaviour. Table 25 shows that almost all estates were making changes to increase enforcement. The main areas that created a sense of disorder, breakdown in controls, and community alienation were all forms of nuisance and disturbance, any form of violence or harassment, property damage, and control of animals. Common nuisance and disturbance were the most frequent problems. In all, over three-quarters of estates had tightened their approach to enforcement, including the use of civil injunctions, protecting witnesses and evicting transgressors.

Links with other agencies

"Sometimes we feel we are taking responsibility for everything which should be dealt with by social services or the police." Local manager

"Social services was cut massively and we lost the local team. Now it's just crisis intervention ... They are sorely missed." Local manager

"Policing is more erratic than any other service." Local manager

"If there is a disturbance, the police overreact with huge vans and go in really heavy with no thought to the community at large." Resident

Housing managers only rarely believed that other agencies were playing a big role on the estates, or having a significant impact on conditions (Figure 27). Schools and voluntary agencies made the greatest contribution; leisure and social services the least. On eight estates no other agency was considered effective. This view reflected the avant-garde position of housing services; it also reflected poor communication and co-ordination between services. It may reflect the beleaguered role of housing managers as they face a widening range of problems with limited resources to respond and poor access to other services.

Table 26 sums up the views of residents and managers on the role of the police, singled out as it was particularly important in 1988 and 1994. In spite of much improved liaison and generally more controlled conditions, both staff and residents were still concerned about policing levels in 1994 and often dissatisfied. Some dissatisfaction may stem from the fear of breakdown resulting from greater pressures and problems. Containing crime and maintaining the improved links were clearly difficult; they did not solve or get rid of the problems, but they did contain them.

Stigma

"I don't tell people where I live." Resident

"I visited some local employers and found that they employed no-one from the estate

Beat police officer and his estate base, London.

Marks left by joyriders, North East.

"Our estate got really good when we had our own policeman – he got to know the kids. I feel sorry for the policemen… so much to do." Resident

because the youth on the estate were thought to be trouble." Local manager

"There is stigma, even within the council, at member level and officer level. We need to bring people here, literally to force them to see the change." Assistant director

Three-quarters of the estates were no longer considered difficult to let and four-fifths were experiencing rising or stable demand, even in areas where demand for other estates was falling (Table 27).

Shifting a chronic lack of demand to other marginal estates by targeting very large sums on certain conspicuous estates could be a huge waste of money. This seemed to have happened in at least three estates in the survey. Most local authorities were not considering the problem of low demand (at least not in the open) from this point of view. Wider evidence of demand

Table 26: **Changes in policing and views on policing**

	Number of estates	
	1988	1994
increased police presence over previous five years	7	0
reduced police presence over previous five years	7	6
insufficient policing	8	10
liaison between police and residents' group	5	15
residents satisfied with policing	na	1
local managers satisfied with policing	10	7

Source: Local managers and residents' groups.

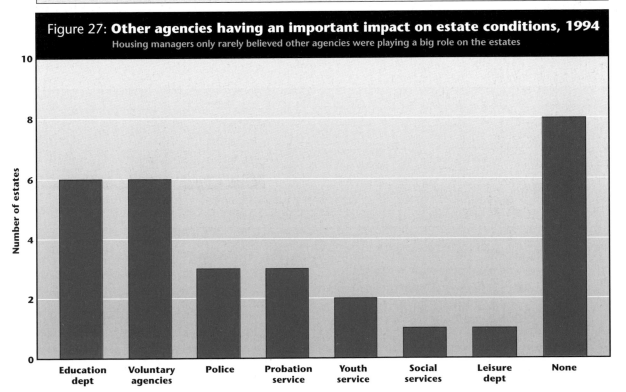

Figure 27: **Other agencies having an important impact on estate conditions, 1994**
Housing managers only rarely believed other agencies were playing a big role on the estates

Source: Local managers.

Table 27: **Demand for estates**

(a) Difficult to let	Start of projects	1982	1988	1994
number of estates	15	9	6	5
(b) Changing demand (1994)	Rising	Stable	Falling	Don't know
number of estates	8	8	2	2

Source: Local, area and senior managers.

problems was not something to which local or central government appeared to pay sufficient attention.

The greater stability of the estates has proved vulnerable to sudden and explosive crises resulting from changes in service levels or lettings policies. Any relaxation in local management control makes unpopular estates highly vulnerable to rapid decline. The underlying stigma has remained in all the estates, though increasingly it may affect only one part or a particular block on the estate severely. Thirteen estates had these enclaves of intense social problems in 1994.

Three residents' groups said that the estates' *reputation* was the worst thing about the estate and another group said, 'we've been vandalised by the media'. Most groups felt that the bad reputation was exaggerated and largely unjustified. Eight estates were still among the least popular in the local authorities. Here residents felt they were discriminated against by hire purchase firms, employers, delivery companies, and insurance. Four estates had changed their names or certain street names to try and overcome this. Stigma was probably the longest-lasting and most deep-seated problem.

6 A change in direction: estate trajectories

Changes in estate conditions between 1980 and 1994

"The three main and interlinked problems still exist - unemployment, poverty ... I don't know what we can do about them, apart from have a sensitive lettings policy and enforce tenancy conditions." Resident

The early impact of local management on estates was strong, visible, and widely recognised. Through the 1980s, in spite of serious polarisation and management problems, a majority of estates continued to improve. In 1994, we measured changes in conditions and management performance in relation to the major problems identified in 1981, although not all changes could be quantified. In important areas it was possible to identify a marked change in the condition of estates and the performance of the local authorities. These changes were matched by an equally noticeable change in the social composition of the estates. This had been one of the dominant issues that in 1979–80 had provoked the estate initiatives. The management performance had in all cases improved, though not always sufficiently or across enough areas of work to have reversed the problem. Table 28 summarises the main changes. The headway made by housing management is clear, despite the persistence or worsening of other problems.

We asked managers and residents for their views of the changes on the estates between the start of the projects and 1994. In 14 cases their views and assessment coincided; in only two cases were opposite views held. In three cases their views were close but not identical. We categorised the changes on estates, based on their views, as: improving; steady or mixed; deteriorating (Table 29). In residents' eyes, 13 estates were either improving or having some success in holding conditions. According to managers, 17 estates were in this position.

Managers' experience in letting the estates and handling tenants' problems, as well as the assessment of area and senior managers covering a far broader area, gave us insight into the changing popularity of estates. We were able to rank the estates in relation to the local authority stock as a whole and in relation to other difficult estates (Figure 28). Thirteen estates had improved in popularity in relation to other estates. Five had kept the same position. Only two were still the worst estates in the local authority.

In spite of improvements, only two estates could now be considered average in terms of popularity with local housing applicants, and none was above average. Compared to other local estates, however, most had improved sufficiently to be ranked higher by senior and local managers than other difficult estates in the area. Whereas in 1981, 16 of the estates were among the least popular in the local authority area, only eight were in that position in 1994.

London balcony estate 1982

"We've come a long way since 1976. When I came here, the fire brigade was out every five minutes with chutes set on fire by the kids, and people were growing marijuana in pots. The west side of the estate was wicked and I was frightened to live here." Resident

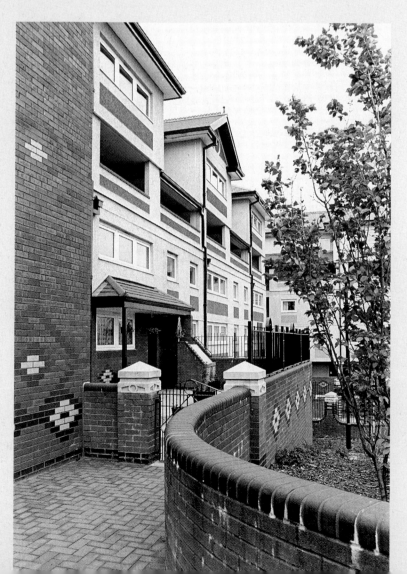

Improvements to blocks remaining after large-scale demolition, North West modern estate 1995

"There is still stigma, even within the council, at member level and at officer level. We need to bring people here, literally to force them to see the change." Assistant director of housing

The most important improvements resulting from the estate projects are summarised in Table 30 under the headings: physical, management and community or resident involvement.

The incidence of positive impacts was almost twice as frequent as mixed impacts. Positive and mixed impacts (with some success and some failure) were overwhelmingly greater than no improvement. The vast majority of estates (at least three-quarters) experienced some positive results from the three central elements of the local initiatives – physical upgrading, management change, and community involvement. Overall, therefore, it was not surprising that our visits in 1994 showed greatly

---

Table 28: Presence of characteristics which led to development of estate-based management

	Number of estates	
	1981	1994
Social composition (compared with local authority)		
higher than average unemployment	16	20
higher than average percentage lone parent households	16	20
higher than average child density	15	20
higher than average ethnic minority	9	10
	Start of project	1994
Conditions affected by local management		
neglected, rubbish-strewn environment	20	1
poor repairs and maintenance	20	7
high levels of crime and vandalism	19	9
higher than local authority average rent arrears	16	13
higher than local authority average voids	14	10
difficult to let	15	5
little resident involvement in management	14	7
Conditions that could not be changed through local management alone		
location	11	11
structural repair	10	6
difficult and unpopular design	7	6
stigma from original slum clearance	6	5

Source: Power (1984), p.8; Census 1981 and 1991; local managers, and residents' groups.

Table 29: Perceptions of changes in estate conditions, 1988–94

	Improving[1]	Steady/mixed[2]	Deteriorating[3]
resident assessment (based on 18 estates)	9	4	5
managers' assessment (based on 20 estates)	10	7	3

Notes:
1 'Improving' denotes continuing improvements over period
2 'Steady/mixed' denotes a levelling off of improvements without a reversion to original levels of problems.
3 'Deteriorating' denotes a marked decline in conditions after initial improvements (early 1980s).
Source: Local managers, and residents.

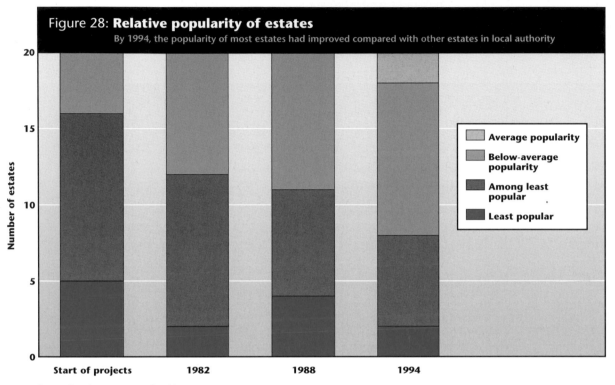

Figure 28: **Relative popularity of estates**
By 1994, the popularity of most estates had improved compared with other estates in local authority

Legend:
- Average popularity
- Below-average popularity
- Among least popular
- Least popular

X-axis: Start of projects, 1982, 1988, 1994
Y-axis: Number of estates

Source: Local managers and residents.

Table 30: **Elements of improvements in estate conditions, 1981–94**

Perceived changes in estate conditions under different elements	Physical	Management	Community/ resident involvement
positive	14	9	11
mixed	5	9	4
no improvement	1	2	5
Total number of estates	20	20	20

Note: Numbers denote estates where the element had each impact.
Source: Local managers and residents.

improved conditions. But any lasting effects of physical upgrading, local management, tenant involvement, and special support happened *in spite of their great social problems* and their generally low status in the eyes of managers and housing applicants. Any gains were gains in a context of growing social difficulty.

Overall direction of change

We then looked at the *overall direction of change* from the perspective of developments, estate by estate, since 1980. Table 31 summarises the direction of change on the estates. The continued progress on ten of the estates was unexpected given the level of social difficulty. We therefore tried to establish how many special forms of support were provided in order to maintain or improve conditions under such difficult circumstances. Table 32 summarises these special supports, showing that in most estates, many different elements were introduced to help residents, to provide more

Table 31: **Direction of change on 20 estates based on evidence from 1982, 1988 and 1994**

Direction of change	Number of estates
improved and still improving	**10**
improved but levelled off – renewed difficulties	**7**
improved then declined	**3**
(of which in crisis – 1)	
(due for demolition – 1)	
Total	**20**

Note: The crisis estate was a Northern cottage estate. The estate due for demolition was a modern London estate. Improved denotes better conditions in 1994 than in 1981 or 1987.
Source: Local managers and residents.

intensive services, to combat extreme conditions, and to alleviate social problems.

These special supports were created and justified, not by central government (though significant funding came partially through DoE, Home Office and so on), but by the local authority landlords. They were a direct response to the intense degradation of estate conditions and their extreme social problems. Without such special measures, the estates would probably have collapsed. Indeed, three estates had already reached a point of no return and were being largely demolished and rebuilt,

in one case entirely. Three others were in the process of dramatic renewal, resulting from extreme crises; in all, at least 13 of the estates had been through a major management crisis which had attracted the special support.

The extreme estate conditions, found in 1980, were again found in 1994, but in a different context, one of local structures and external support. The sustainability of the improvements hinged directly on the most fundamental two elements of change: the creation of local service structures and the continuation of external support. This was evidenced by the rapid and renewed crisis when support and special status were withdrawn. Seven estates had gone through a renewed crisis over the period, when external support and local inputs were reduced.

The intensified polarisation made self-sustaining improvements unlikely or impossible, and made steady trajectories of progress highly dependent on continued outside intervention and special support. Conditions on estates had only improved and been sustained through radical changes in the way estate problems were tackled. It was not more of the same, but a total change in direction.

Table 32: **Special supports or unusual factors helping to maintain improvements**

Special features	Number of estates with feature
special security measures	**19**
extra capital investment	**16**
higher staff/dwellings ratios	**15**
special community facilities	**14**
fewer units per local office[1]	**13**
political and senior officer support	**11**
strong tenant leadership	**7**
special tenant liaison and council links[2]	**6**
special support worker, e.g. community development	**5**

Notes:
1 Compared with other local offices within local authority.
2 More direct links to council and more support than other areas.
Source: Based on local and senior managers' views, 1994.

Table 33: **Main changes that affected estate trajectories**

Important changes	Number of estates
special outside support and locally-based change	**19**
local authority intensive estate-based management[1]	**17**
local authority estate improvements	**17**
dramatic redesign and physical/structural change	**7**
partial demolition – under 15%	**5**
partial sale - under 20%	**4**
tenant control or major tenant influence through localised structures	**4**
estate demolition – over 90%	**1**

Note: 1 Originally 20; two offices now closed; one moved off estate to cover wider area.
Source: Authors' assessment.

Common elements in change

The changes took many different forms. Table 33 summarises the most important. There were several elements common to all estates to varying degrees:

- special initiatives to counter intense decline;
- continuing special focus of effort (which ended in two cases by the late 1980s);
- targeted capital spending;
- localised services;
- tenant involvement.

These elements could be applied to any estate with intense problems. They would not eradicate the problems. They would contain them, thereby making conditions more acceptable. Box A summarises the three main factors affecting the estates.

There was a constant tension on most estates between the pressures created by different characteristics. The unchangeable and difficult to change characteristics exercised a downward and negative pressure on the local factors that were more susceptible to change. But residents, landlords and government responded to the need for action and tackled elements that could be changed more easily, thereby limiting the downward spiral of estate conditions.

Box A: **Factors affecting estates**

Unchangeable characteristics
Location:
- periphery
- depressed region
- poor urban area

Difficult to change characteristics
Requiring major capital expenditure
- type of estate
- size of estate
- estate features, e.g. towers, decks
- unit sizes
Government policies
- tenure structure
- polarisation and the growing marginalisation of estates
- poverty trap and dependence
Wider economic and social currents requiring major restructuring
- unemployment and poverty
- discrimination and racial concentrations
- family change and lone parenthood

Local characteristics that can be changed
- housing management organisation
- delivery of other local services
- tenant liaison and participation
- local activities and facilities
- links with voluntary groups and other services

7

Conclusions and recommendations

Exceptional estates?

- The 20 unpopular estates that pioneered local housing management from 1980 were at the extreme end of difficult-to-manage rented council housing. But they shared many of their difficult characteristics with 2,000 other council estates and with many newer housing association estates.[46] They were not *uniquely* difficult, in their scale, near-uniform tenure, or disadvantage.

- By the time of our visits in 1994, most of the 20 estates were no longer the least popular in their areas. *Large, publicly subsidised, low-income, single use, rented estates generally face serious social and management problems on a major scale.*

Local focus

- Local services were as important as physical reinvestment in improving conditions. For example, better street cleaning or caretaking, better repairs, or fully occupied properties improved the estates for everyone in the same way as environmental improvement or better security. *Intensive estate-based management and reinvestment, focused on particularly difficult estates, appeared to have arrested decline.*

- One of the great advantages of area improvements and localised services was that they raised the *general* standards of an estate, making the estate as an area more acceptable. *The focus on an estate or area therefore emerged as pivotal to success.*

Hands-on management

- The estate bases provided hands-on control, direct contact with problems, and the ability to respond to pressure. *Estates with a local office were easier to manage and better for residents.*

- Sustained effort – dating from 1980 or before, to 1994 and beyond – was the key to progress. However, the management task was the management of poor conditions – public support alongside private poverty. No matter how high the quality of local services, the gap in income between estate residents and average households did not change fundamentally. *The social pressures on the local management service were intensifying due to the growing concentrations of disadvantage.*

Management control

- As social pressures increased over the late 1980s and early 1990s, so local management control tightened, in order to avert renewed decay. Housing management could not work on its own. Estates required a *combination of physical, social, and management measures.*

Location and demand

- Most cities in the survey were losing population. The estates were in declining and disadvantaged inner city areas, or on the periphery of cities. In some cases, there was simply too much housing in the wrong places.

- *Inner city estates* were in some ways easier to restore than outer estates. They were closer to shops, transport, jobs and other services. But breaking up these estates and blending them into the urban surroundings was always expensive and difficult. *They often continue to stand out as 'council housing' even after exceptional spending to integrate them.*

- *Outer estates*, while physically attractive, usually remained isolated, poor and vulnerable, with low demand, a strong stigma, many social, family and crime problems. Location makes their links with the city weak and hard to strengthen.

Demolition

- *Demolition* was increasingly on the agenda as the simplest way out of ugly estate structures and low demand, including in parts of London. But it was the most expensive option of all, highly disruptive, and leads to a *significant loss of low income housing. Changing use, occupancy and tenure patterns were cheaper and more constructive alternatives. This was possible without uprooting whole populations.*

Benefit dependence

- Rapid economic change, changes in social and family patterns, tenure change, and two extended, deep recessions since 1980 had led to increasing reliance on the welfare system. The estates epitomised benefit dependence in intensely concentrated form. *Most people on the estates depended on state benefits.*
- People found it very difficult to get work that set them free from benefit dependence and gave them sufficient incentives to risk losing benefits. *Some blurring of the line between benefits and low-paid part-time casual work –* the type of work normally available to estate residents – *seemed essential.*[47]
- The economic changes of the last twenty years affecting estates in an extreme way are part of a world-wide, deep-set and long-term

pattern.[48] Local housing management is only *a small beginning to a much bigger process that will be essential to the survival of the estates under threat of disintegration at the extreme edges of society.*

Joblessness

- The shortage of jobs in the estates was chronic. Many households – even young ones – had lost all connection with the job market. The poverty trap separated unemployed people from the few opportunities there were. Informal work and the black economy were supposed to flourish in some areas but it was unclear whether this really worked in estates where there were few local employers, where people were cut off from almost any economic activity, and where residents *normally* did not work. *Having a job of any kind was seen by many residents as an elusive goal.*

Discrimination

- Three groups, experiencing greater poverty and social disadvantage than most, have grown significantly over fifteen years on the estates – the jobless, lone-parent families, and minority ethnic households. On most estates, over 60 per cent of adult residents had no work; the proportion of lone-parent headed households was *over four* times the national average; and on several London estates, members of minority ethnic groups formed a majority of households.
- Social disadvantage and wider discrimination exclude households with weak choice in housing or jobs markets from other areas or tenures, resulting in *social housing estates generally* (and no longer only these extreme examples) becoming more polarised. The status of social housing has fallen as a result. The over-concentration of disadvantage in these estates made stigma lasting. *The special*

initiatives on estates helped people who otherwise would have suffered the triple handicap of social discrimination, economic disadvantage, and significantly inferior housing conditions.

- Racial discrimination was a major issue. When once patterns of area segregation become permanent and expectations are fixed, it is very difficult to break them. *Separate areas for discriminated against groups quickly become rejected enclaves from which escape is difficult and in which conditions become inherently unequal. Separate rarely means equal.*

Mitigating polarising effects

- The impact of polarisation was mitigated by upgraded conditions, by tenant involvement, social activities, more facilities, stronger enforcement and more security measures. But there was scope – and urgent need – for far greater action on a much broader front. For example, school failure was a concern to many parents. *Innovative educational programmes could transform opportunity for estate children, often handicapped by low educational achievement.*[49]
- Secondary schools serving disadvantaged areas should possibly be smaller and organised with a stronger commitment to *usable education.*

Work and economic change

- *New economic patterns* may be emerging on estates where organisations like credit unions and other self-help activities are becoming popular in reaction to greater poverty. The local estate base, capital works, cleaning, caretaking, repairs, patrolling, and tenant activities all created action on estates. Further localisation of services such as police, health, and social services, could mean over 100 jobs per estate.[50] The localisation of services potentially creates spin-offs for

estates by diversifying functions, generating activity, bringing people from outside into the area, generating demand for shops and buses, localising money circulation, and inevitably creating more work for local people. *The greater the level of local activity, the more secure and supervised an estate becomes and the more local people experience normal conditions.*

Local service jobs

- Professional skills and central support are extremely important in making local services work. But so are *direct service jobs.* Estates need many more of the latter and possibly rather less of the former. The jobs that make a difference to estate conditions are mainly local jobs. It is possible to fund two jobs at the front line for one job in the Town Hall, as central overheads shrink.[51] On estates, the balance seems to have tipped too far away from the kind of custodial presence, on-going maintenance and direct contact jobs that keep densely built-up and occupied areas habitable. This general loss of direct service jobs on estates hits residents badly, not least in employment opportunities but also in estate conditions, estate security and supervision. The 20 estates had more locally-based staff than average but *most large estates still do not have many essential services locally-based.*

Training for work

- *The creation of more part-time, short-term work through the localised services might expand the supply of local jobs and enhance the chances of young people getting some experience of employment and therefore some links to the job market.* This would help generate a new atmosphere of progress. A more positive emphasis on training and trainee posts would help. *A training strategy will only succeed if accompanied by significant support.*

71

Tenant involvement and estate conditions

- The critical role of residents in successful estate initiatives is now part of the conventional housing wisdom. It is widely accepted as central to success. Tenants' stake in their homes and neighbourhood, their local knowledge, experience of estate problems, and personal investment in any improvements gives them a sharp perspective on priorities, on what does and does not work, on where the problems lie. Tenants can also have a major role in helping to control conditions and are deeply frustrated by loss of control. *The continuing hold of local management on estate conditions was extremely important to resident organisations and their representatives.*

- Tenant involvement in local initiatives, in spite of obvious limitations, greatly affected the morale of the community and of the local staff. It brought disproportionate gains. *'Direct democracy' at the estate level was important, not just for residents but for the vitality of democracy as a whole.* It was one way of countering the impact of polarisation and giving people a chance to communicate directly with those on whom they depended. It therefore made self-reliance more likely.

- Over the fifteen years of estate-based management, the role of tenants had grown. Resident organisations had come to represent a *lynch-pin in the improvement process.*

- Only in the case of tenant management organisations did control shift radically in favour of residents and this only worked with exceptional leadership and support. *Most tenants' groups did not feel able to take on responsibility for difficult areas.*

- Tenants were concerned by the increasing social pressures on estates. Fear of social breakdown made them anxious about policing, security and even further

polarisation. Tenants were less optimistic than managers, due to a greater feeling of powerlessness.

- More emphasis was needed on social and economic elements of estate life. Extending the role of residents, expanding their opportunities for learning, *involving them in schools, training, policing, health, social services, environmental issues*, could serve to reshape those other services in the way that it had housing.

- Resident involvement in the organisation and development of services on which they depend reduces the divide between providers (in work, with money) and users (in this case usually out of work with little money). Support and training help to develop responsible, effective leadership and create viable local organisations.

- Residents became members of many different, more or less formal groups. We found a lot of *unpaid work and activity* that harkened back to a semi-subsistence economy. *Residents were often active with a minimum of cash exchange.*

Lettings

- Lettings policies and their impact on estates caused serious concern. Coercive, centralised lettings policies damage community relations. Encouraging families and friends to stay near each other, and introducing an element of choice, are important in otherwise difficult-to-let communities.

Policing

- The police could only operate with the community's support. To be really effective they needed a strong local presence and a redeployment of resources from bureaucratic and centralised structures out to estates and streets. Without a local base, it was hard for the police to balance their roles in responding to calls from older, more established residents, and in maintaining positive community links.

- The threat of ungovernable conditions made the presence of the police crucial to basic order. In one of the estates, the local police had insufficient presence or authority to contain or prevent breakdown. On the other estates, a well-organised local presence with community support had a big impact. *Security and crime conditions were being held steady on most estates in spite of greatly increased social problems.*

- *Young people* were more numerous on these estates than generally. They were volatile, under-occupied, attracted by groups, by excitement and by alternative anti-authority attitudes. They committed most of the crime. Listening to young people, involving them in estate matters, developing with them a sense of the future was critically important, but an under-developed area of work. *Unless local leaders have links both with young people and the police, the situation can easily explode, as it had on three estates.*

Sustainable improvements

- Estate decline was so severe that major injections of improvement capital and community support were necessary. Layers of government initiatives over the 1980s favoured these estates and most of them experienced significant *short-term physical* improvement programmes. This was *no substitute* for continuing local management for which *no 'exit strategy' can or should be devised.* Just as a school needs local teachers as well as a broader education service, rented estates need *local* landlord services funded from rent income as well as wider programmes, policies, and support.

- Spending on the stock of social housing, now ageing and often reaching the point of replacement, needs to be *structured in a more*

rational, long-term and planned manner, avoiding some of the 'swing-boat' effects of reinvestment policies.

- We concluded that the only way to sustain estate conditions was to *generalise the lessons of intensive management and to tackle all large, concentrated, low-income, rented estates in a similar, focused way,* applying the lessons to as many services as possible.

The impact of government policies

- Some government housing strategies in the 1980s made a positive impact on estates. *Tenant involvement, ring-fencing of housing revenue budgets and accounts, Estate Action and localised management were largely positive.* They won the support of housing departments and residents and achieved real change.

- Other policies had a much more mixed outcome. The Right to Buy distributed benefits extremely unevenly between estates and left most of the 20 estates still overwhelmingly council-owned and *therefore significantly more polarised in 1994 than in 1980.* The move to 'flagship' projects and high profile spending through City Challenge and Housing Action Trust programmes consumed large resources that were too narrowly focused, *making the introduction of planned reinvestment and steady maintenance less likely.*

- The impacts of Compulsory Competitive Tendering for housing management and the Single Regeneration Budget have yet to emerge. These are by far the most significant new policy initiatives, offering *potentially more streamlined services, more broad-based and co-ordinated spending and a more firmly localised partnership approach to regeneration.* But the combination of economic pressures, public spending cuts and the loss of status and morale in many local authorities could hamper progress.

73

- Estates may no longer receive the local focus they need, either through CCT management contracts involving bigger areas or through SRB refurbishment with less money for estates. Both policies may reduce the role of residents. *The aim of breaking away from estate isolation will not be achieved by a reduction in effort to tackle estate problems. Both CCT and SRB are diluting effort at estate level.*

Europe

- The European experience of social housing estates is relevant to our conclusions. Northern European Union members have many similar large, separate, social housing estates. They are generally owned by independent landlords, subject to less direct political control or intervention, and managed with far more intensive, localised custodial and maintenance services. They focus less on welfare and more on financial viability. Their management is tighter and standards higher. They rely on *partnership* with local authorities.
- Nonetheless they are experiencing a similar underlying trend towards social polarisation, high concentrations of need, falling popularity, and management difficulty. They too have engaged in special reinvestment programmes, localised management and resident involvement. *These programmes have had a measurable impact on conditions on the Continent.*[52] But marginal social housing estates may symbolise a deep rift in Western societies between the dominant and the disadvantaged.

Conclusion

The housing market and the competitive economy push people with less resources or skills to the bottom. The social commitment to provide shelter pushes those who fail towards the lowest point in the hierarchy of provision.

The least popular estates are a large scale and inadequate solution to a recurring problem. Maintaining conditions through careful, on-going management, paid for out of rents, offers an incremental, multi-faceted strategy that has succeeded in some of the most extreme conditions. It can surely therefore succeed in other areas.

Recommendations

- It is important to protect what works, in areas which are highly vulnerable.
- Localisation should be extended to other estates without local management and to other services on estates.
- Improved local services should be used to bridge the gap between estate communities and other parts of the urban area. This equalising force may be vital to urban stability.
- A focus on cities as dynamic entities, where there is plentiful infrastructure, makes sense. Breaking out from 'the estate' concept and linking estates to cities are important new directions for urban policy. But the special needs of estates must not be overlooked.
- A balance needs to be struck between local, organic development – bottom up – and planned outside support and investment – top down. *Both* are necessary.
- Spending programmes on estates should build in incentives for resident training and involvement, and long-term maintenance and management; they should operate on a longer, more flexible time-scale. Capital should sometimes be replaced by revenue.
- Regional housing supply and demand must be assessed at a level *above* local authorities in order to analyse the competing claims of different providers and to prevent 'resource and initiative grabbing'. Slack demand should signal a brake on subsides for further building.

- Work has become so much scarcer that it must be shared if more people are to move out of dependence.
- The changing, more 'enabling', role of local authorities could be used creatively in advancing ideas for localisation of more services.
- Avoiding the formation of social and racial ghettos should receive the highest political priority. We urgently need new thinking on city problems.
- Families, children and young people on estates are vulnerable to many pressures. New thinking and new priority must be given to protecting and supporting them.
- Cities are youthful and have large ethnic populations. These groups offer vitality, energy, enterprise and they should be fostered, as part of society, not as separate problems.

The rising tide of polarisation, creating even greater concentrations of social problems in certain unpopular estates, undermines confidence among residents and staff. But the continuing estate initiatives lasting from around 1980 to 1994 had brought real progress to most estates. The constant effort, attention to detail, local networks and external support were like swimming against the tide. By dint of strong, continual energetic action, it proved possible to make progress against the undertow.

Appendix tables

Table A1: Visits and interviews carried out 1982–94

	1981	1987	1994
estate visits	40	60	84
resident interviews	5 individuals	15 groups	17 groups
		54 individuals	131 individuals
local/neighbourhood manager interviews	20	20[1]	20[1]
area/district manager interviews	0	0	9
director/assistant director interviews[2]	18	18	14
other estate-based worker interviews, e.g. police, community workers, youth workers	0	0	16

Notes:
1 Where there was no local office and manager, the housing officer with most knowledge about the estate was interviewed.
2 The twenty estates are located in eighteen local authorities.

Table A2: Details of the 20 estates

Region	Local authority	Date built	Estate size (units)	Date project started	Size of area covered by local office in 1994 (units)
Cottage					
North West	**Bolton**	1930s	473	1980	1,608
North East	**Gateshead**[1]	1940s, 50s	1,000	1980	993
East Midlands	**Leicester**	1930s	1,975	1981	1,700
North East	**Newcastle**[1]	1920s, 30s	1,000	1978	1,600
North East	**Stockton**	1940s	393	1981	500
North West	**Tameside**	1930s	312	1981	2,800
West Midlands	**Walsall**	1930s	350	1982	420
Balcony					
Inner London	**Hackney**[2]	1950s	698	1979	4,100
Inner London	**Islington**[2]	1949	559	1978	2,500
Inner London	**Lambeth**	1930s	888	1980	1,820
Inner London	**Lewisham**	1930s	1,350	1979	1,500
North West	**Liverpool**	1930s, 50s, 60s	1,930	1979	1,550
Outer London	**Wandsworth**	1930s	272	1981	5,000
Modern					
Outer London	**Brent**	1960s	1,849	1976	1,800
Inner London	**Greenwich**	1970s	1,898	1980	2,500
Inner London	**Hammersmith and Fulham**	1970s	812	1979	
Inner London	**Haringey**	1970s	1,063	1981	1,063
Inner London	**Lambeth**	1970s	1,500	1979	1,700
Inner London	**Lewisham**	1960s	1,114	1978	1,300
North West	**Rochdale**	1960s, 70s	1,014	1981	2,500

Notes:
1 A few flats.
2 A few tall blocks.

Table A3: Socio-economic change 1981–91: summary (characteristics of population, %)

		Residents of Great Britain	Residents of the eighteen local authority areas	Residents of the twenty estates
unemployed[1]	1981	9	11	28
	1991	10	13	34
economically inactive[2]	1981	39	37	39
	1991	36	37	44
under 16s	1981	21	21	31
	1991	19	20	31
under 24s	1981	37	37	50
	1991	33	34	46
pensioners[3]	1981	18	17	13
	1991	18	16	11
minority ethnic	1981[4]	4	9	21
	1991[5]	6	19	26
lone parent headed households	1981	3	3	9
	1991	4	6	18

Notes:
1 Registered unemployed residents as a proportion of economically active residents aged sixteen and over.
2 Economically inactive residents as a proportion of residents aged sixteen and over – including those over retirement age.
3 Residents over retirement age – 60 for women, 65 for men – as a proportion of all residents.
4 Residents living in households headed by a person born in the New Commonwealth as a proportion of all residents.
5 Residents defined by the head of household as being of minority ethnicity as a proportion of all residents.
Source: Census, 1981 and 1991.

Table A4: Population change in study local authorities 1971-91 (%)

Local authority	1971–81	1981–91	Local authority	1971–81	1981–91
North West			London		
Bolton	+0.5	–2.5	Hackney	–18.0	–10.0
Tameside	–2.0	–2.6	Islington	–21.0	–4.3
Rochdale	+2.0	–4.5	Haringey	–15.0	–8.9
			Brent	–10.0	–10.1
North East			Hammersmith and Fulham	–21.0	–7.5
Newcastle	–10.0	–7.5	Lambeth	–20.0	–11.3
Gateshead	–6.0	–7.1	Lewisham	–3.0	–7.3
Stockton-on-Tees	+5.0	–0.6	Greenwich	–3.0	–5.6
Midlands			national average	+1.0	+2.5
Walsall	–3.0	–3.9			
Leicester	–	–5.0	Source: Census, 1981 and 1991.		
Merseyside					
Liverpool	–26.0	–13.5			

Table A5: **Capital investment funding, 1980–94**

	Number of estates receiving funding from each source			
	Total	Cottage	Balcony	Modern
local authority Housing Investment Programme	20	7	6	7
Urban Programme	13	3	4	6
Estate Action	9	1	1	7
City Challenge	5	1	2	2
Safer Cities	3	–	1	2
Inner Cities Task Force	3	1	1	1
private sector	2	1	–	1
Housing Association Grant	3	1	2	–
Single Regeneration Budget	0	–	–	–

Source: Local and area managers.

Table A6: **Organisation of repairs services (number of estates)**

	Central repairs service only[1]	Decentralised repairs service		
		Serving wider area than estate	Serving estate only	All
(a) Number with each organisation				
1982	2	10	8	20
1988	7	9	4	20
1994	–	13	7	20
(b) Performance in 1994 (over last two years)				
improved	–	5	2	7
same	–	4	2	6
deteriorated	–	4	2	6
don't know	–	–	1	1

Note:
1 All central repairs services carried out specialised work in all estates throughout the period, and in many cases also emergency work.
Source: Local managers and residents.

Table A7: **Management and repair costs, 1993/94 (£/week per unit)**

(a) Management (12 estates)
    estate-based unit management cost (staff costs only)   **£2.87**
    local authority unit management costs (including local and central management costs)   **£13.58**

(b) Repair[1] (10 estates)
    estates   **£9.44**
    local authority average   **£9.11**

Note:
1 Day-to-day repair costs, not including repairs to voids prior to letting. There was a lack of clear local repairs information on half the estates.
Source: Local managers and housing department annual reports 1993/94.

Table A8: **Take-up of the "Right to Buy" 1980–94 (%)**

	Homes bought as a percentage of the 1980 stock	
	Estates	Study local authorities
all	**5.0**	**19[1]**
cottage	**5.0**	**na**
balcony	**6.3**	**na**
modern	**3.4**	**na**

Note:
1 National average take-up is 26 per cent.

Notes

1 Power (1991b).

2 Burbidge et al. (1981).

3 Department of the Environment (1981).

4 Osborne and Gaebler (1992).

5 Power (1984).

6 Mainwaring (1988).

7 Wilmott and Murie (1988); Hills (1995), Figs 9 and 49.

8 For example, Prime Minister Margaret Thatcher at the Conservative Party annual conference in 1987; Murray (1990); G. Turner, 'Despair and the semtex factor', the *Daily Mail*, 27th July 1992; P. Victor et al., 'Fear rules in no-go Britain', the *Independent on Sunday*, 17th April, 1994; Smith (1993).

9 The initial visits were recorded in reports presented to the Secretary of State for the Environment, to the Department of the Environment, and to the Greater London Council between 1979 and 1982. Developments in the estates between these early visits and 1982 are recorded and analysed in Power (1984), and those between 1982 and 1988 in Power (1991a).

10 Moser and Peake (1987).

11 Power (1993; forthcoming).

12 1983 local authority Housing Investment Programme returns to the DoE on councils' 'difficult to let' housing.

13 Burbidge et al. (1981).

14 Estate Action annual reports (1985–93).

15 Power (1984), p. 8.

16 Power (1984), p. 32.

17 Power (1991b), pp. 19–26.

18 Power (1991a).

19 Glennerster and Turner (1993).

20 Census, 1981 and 1991.

21 Department of the Environment/Scottish Office/Welsh Office (1981).

22 Central Statistical Office (1994).

23 Wilmott and Murie (1988).

24 Wilson (1987); Jencks and Peterson (1990).

25 Hills (1993), Fig. 17; Hills (1995), Fig. 30.

26 Hills (1995), Fig. 43.

27 Green (1994).

28 Hills (1995), Figs 3, 4 and 7.

29 Hough and Mayhew (1983); Mayhew et al. (1989, 1993).

30 Commission for Racial Equality (1988; 1989).

31 Commission for Racial Equality (1989).

32 Greater London Council (1976).

33 Power (1987a), p. 49.

34 Greater London Council (1976); Cullingworth (1979).

35 General Household Survey 1991.

36 Forrest and Murie (1991).

37 White (1946).

38 CHAC (1939, 1945, 1959).

39 Crossman (1975).

40 Power (1987a); Dunleavy (1981).

41 Greater London Council (1976).

42 LCC (1937).

43 Burbidge et al. (1981).

44 Power (1987).

45 For example, Coleman (1985); Hillier (1988); Ravetz (1988).

46 Power (1994); see also Page (1993).

47 Barclay (1995), pp. 48–50.

48 Reich (1993).

49 Atkinson (1993).

50 Power (1992).

51 Power (1987b; 1991a; forthcoming).

52 Power (forthcoming).

References

Atkinson, D (1993): *Radical Urban Alternatives.* London: Cassell

Barclay, P (1995) (Chairman): *Income and Wealth Volume 1.* York: Joseph Rowntree Foundation

Burbidge, M et al. (1981): *An Investigation of Difficult to Let Housing. Vol. 1 General findings; Vol. 2 Case studies of post-war estates; Vol. 3 Case studies of pre-war estates.* London: Department of the Environment

Central Statistical Office (1994): *Social Trends.* London: HMSO

CHAC [Housing management sub-committee of the Central Housing Advisory Committee of the Ministry of Housing and Local Government] (1939): *Management of Municipal Housing Estates: First report.* London: HMSO

CHAC (1945): *Management of Municipal Housing Estates: Second report.* London: HMSO

CHAC (1959): *Councils and their Houses: Eighth report.* London: HMSO

Coleman, A (1985): *Utopia on Trial: Vision and reality in planned housing.* London: Hilary Shipman

Commission for Racial Equality (1988): *Homelessness and Discrimination: Report of a formal investigation into the London Borough of Tower Hamlets.* London: CRE

Commission for Racial Equality (1989): *Race, Housing and Immigration: A guide.* London: CRE

Crossman, R (1975): *The Diaries of a Cabinet Minster Vol. 1.* London: Hamish Hamilton and Jonathan Cape

Cullingworth, J B (1979): *Essays on Housing Policy: The British scene.* London: Allen & Unwin

Department of the Environment (1981): *Priority Estates Project 1981: Improving problem council estates.* London: HMSO

Department of the Environment (1983): *English House Condition Survey 1981: Part 1 Report of the physical condition survey.* London: DoE

Department of the Environment (1991): *Index of Local Conditions.* London: DoE

Department of the Environment (1993): *English House Condition Survey: 1991: Preliminary report on unfit dwellings.* London: DoE

Department of the Environment/Scottish Office/Welsh Office (1981): *Housing and Construction Statistics 1970–80.* London: HMSO

Dunleavy, P (1981): *The Politics of Mass Housing in Britain 1945–75.* Oxford: Clarendon Press

Estate Action (1985–94): *Estate Action Annual Report.* London: DoE

Forrest, R and Murie, A (1991): *Selling the Welfare State: The privatisation of public housing.* London: Routledge

Glennerster, H and Turner, T (1993): *Estate Based Housing Management: An evaluation.* London: HMSO

Greater London Council (1976): *Colour and the Allocation of GLC Housing: Report of the GLC lettings survey 1974–75.* London: GLC

Green, A (1994): *The Geography of Poverty and Wealth.* Warwick: Institute for Employment Research, University of Warwick

Hillier, B (1988): 'Against enclosure' in Teymur, N et al. (eds) *Rehumanizing Housing.* London: Butterworths

Hills, J (1993): *The Future of Welfare: A guide to the debate.* York: Joseph Rowntree Foundation

Hills, J (1995): *Income and Wealth Volume 2: A summary of the evidence.* York: Joseph Rowntree Foundation

Hope, T and Foster, J (1993): *Housing, Community and Crime: The impact of the Priority Estates Project.* Home Office Research Study No.131. London: HMSO

Hough, M and Mayhew, P (1983): *The British Crime Survey: first report.* Home Office Research Study No. 76. London: HMSO

Jencks, C and Peterson, P E (eds.) (1990): *The Urban Underclass.* Washington DC: The Brookings Institution

LCC [London County Council] (1937): *London Housing*. London: LCC

Mainwaring, R (1988): *The Walsall Experience: a study of the decentralisation of Walsall's housing service*. London: HMSO

Mayhew, P et al. (1989): *The 1988 British Crime Survey*. Home Office Research Study No. 111. London: HMSO

Mayhew, P et al. (1993): *The 1992 British Crime Survey*. Home Office Research Study No. 132. London: HMSO

Moser, C and Peake, L (eds) (1987): *Women, Human Settlements and Housing*. London: Tavistock

Murray, C (1990): *The Emerging British Underclass*. London: Institute for Economic Affairs Health and Welfare Unit

Osborne, D and Gaebler, T (1992): *Reinventing Government*. Reading, MA: Addison-Wesley

Page, D (1993): *Building for Communities: A study of new housing association estates*. York: Joseph Rowntree Foundation

Power, A (1984): *Local Housing Management: A Priority Estates Project survey*. London: DoE

Power, A (1987a): *Property before People: The management of twentieth-century council housing*. London: Allen & Unwin

Power, A (1987b): *The PEP Guide to Local Housing Management, Vols. 1, 2, 3*. London: Department of the Environment

Power, A (1991a): *Running to Stand Still: Progress in local management on twenty unpopular housing estates*. London: PEP

Power, A (1991b): *Housing Management: A guide to quality and creativity*. London: Longman Group

Power, A 1992): *Empowering Residents*. Report of OECD Conference, Edinburgh, 1992: OECD

Power, A (1993): *Hovels to High Rise: State housing in Europe since 1850*. London: Routledge

Power, A (1994): *Area-Based Poverty, Social Problems and Resident Empowerment*. Welfare State Programme WSP/107 Suntory-Toyota International Centre for Economics and Related Disciplines, LSE, London

Power, A (forthcoming): *Chaos or Community: The social consequences of mass housing in Northern Europe*

Ravetz, A (1988): 'Malaise, design and history: scholarship and experience on trial' in Teymur, N et al. (eds) *Rehumanizing Housing*. London: Butterworths

Reich, R (1993): *The Work of Nations: Preparing ourselves for 21st century capitalism*. New York: Vintage Books

Smith, D (1993): *Understanding the Underclass*. London: Policy Studies Institute

White, L (1946): *Tenement Town*. London: Jason Press

Wilson, J (1987): *The Truly Disadvantaged*. Chicago: University of Chicago Press

Willmott, P and Murie, A (1988): *Polarisation and Social Housing: the British and French experience*. London: PSI

List of figures and tables

List of figures

Figure 1 Residents interviewed in 1994 *p11*

Figure 2 Average number of homes by type of estate *p13*

Figure 3 Location of the 20 estates, showing building type *p14*

Figure 4 Outline patterns of social decline on estates *p15*

Figure 5 Unemployment 1981 and 1991 *p18*

Figure 6 Economic inactivity 1981 and 1991 *p19*

Figure 7 Employment in 1981 and 1991 *p20*

Figure 8 Unemployment by estate and local authority 1981 and 1991 *p21*

Figure 9 Proportion of young people on estates and nationally 1981 and 1991 *p23*

Figure 10 Elderly population 1981 and 1991 *p24*

Figure 11 Lone parents 1981 and 1991 *p24*

Figure 12 Lone parent headed households by estate and local authority *p26*

Figure 13 Minority ethnic population by estate and local authority 1981 and 1991 *p27*

Figure 14 GCSE performance 1994 *p29*

Figure 15 A level performance 1994 *p30*

Figure 16 Absence from school 1994 *p31*

Figure 17 Tenure structure 1981 and 1991/94 *p33*

Figure 18 Tenure on estates by type of estate 1994 *p33*

Figure 19 Tenure by estate, 1994 *p35*

Figure 20 Changes in functions covered by local offices *p41*

Figure 21 Specialised staff in local offices 1994 *p42*

Figure 22 Average number of callers in local offices 1994 *p43*

Figure 23 Empty properties on five 'lettings crisis' estates *p45*

Figure 24 Local lettings and empty properties *p46*

Figure 25 'One-offer' policies and voids *p46*

Figure 26 Severity of crime problems by type of estate 1994 *p58*

Figure 27 Other agencies having an important impact on estate conditions 1994 *p61*

Figure 28 Relative popularity of estates *p66*

List of tables

Table 1 Size, style and age of the 20 estates *p12*

Table 2 Location of estates by design *p14*

Table 3 Study local authority population change 1971–91 *p17*

Table 4 Capital works 1988–94, on 20 estates *p38*

Table 5 Average number of physical measures taken to tackle problems by type of estate 1988–94 *p39*

Table 6 Average cost per unit of capital works 1988–94 *p39*

Table 7 Managers' and residents' assessment of capital works, 1988-94 *p40*

Table 8 Number of estates with budgets *p42*

Table 9 Average number of homes covered by local offices *p42*

Table 10 Ratio of properties to staff *p43*

Table 11 Empty properties 1980–94 *p43*

Table 12 Turnover of estate population 1982–94 *p47*

Table 13 Average rent levels in the local authorities with the 20 estates 1982–94 *p47*

Table 14 Rent arrears 1982–94 *p47*

Table 15 Impact of localised housing benefit service on arrears performance 1994 (average number of weeks' rent owing) *p48*

Table 16 Structure and assessment of caretaking service by type of estate 1994 *p50*

Table 17 Frequency of meetings between council staff and residents' groups 1994 *p51*

Table 18 Types and numbers of residents' organisations on estates 1982–1994 *p53*

Table 19 Support for residents' groups *p54*

Table 20 Problems facing residents' groups, according to managers 1994 *p56*

Table 21 Activities and services available in the estates *p56*

Table 22 Estate and neighbourhood facilities 1994 *p57*

Table 23 Types of crime and anti-social behaviour occurring on estates, 1994 *p57*

Table 24 Perceptions of change in crime level, 1988–94 *p58*

Table 25 Changes to tenancy agreements to increase power of enforcement 1988-94 *p59*

Table 26 Changes in policing and views on policing *p61*

Table 27 Demand for estates *p62*

Table 28 Presence of characteristics which led to development of estate-based management *p65*

Table 29 Perceptions of changes in estate conditions 1988–94 *p65*

Table 30 Elements of improvements in estate conditions 1981–94 *p66*

Table 31 Direction of change on 20 estates based on evidence from 1982, 1988 and 1994 *p67*

Table 32 Special supports or unusual factors helping to maintain improvements *p67*

Table 33 Main changes that affected estate trajectories *p68*

Appendix tables

Table A1 Visits and interviews carried out 1982–94 *p76*

Table A2 Details of the 20 estates *p76*

Table A3 Socio-economic change 1981–91 *p77*

Table A4 Population change in study local authorities, 1971-91 *p77*

Table A5 Capital investment funding, 1980–94 *p78*

Table A6 Organisation of repairs services *p78*

Table A7 Management and repair costs, 1993/94 *p79*

Table A8: Take-up of the 'Right to Buy' 1980–94 *p79*